The Children's Year

crafts and clothes for children and parents to make

by

Stephanie Cooper

Christine Fynes-Clinton

Marye Rowling

Hawthorn Press

"Joy in living, a love for all existence, energy for work – such are among the life-long results of a right cultivation of the feeling for beauty and for art. The relationship of man to man, how noble, how beautiful it becomes under this influence! Again, the moral sense, which is also being formed in the child during these years through the pictures of life that are placed before him, through the authorities to whom he looks up – this moral sense becomes assured, if the child out of his own sense of beauty feels the good to be at the same time beautiful, the bad to be at the same time ugly."

From 'The Education of the Child in the Light of Anthroposophy' by Rudolf Steiner.

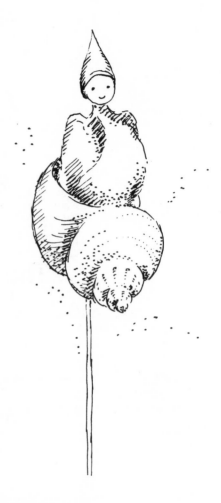

Acknowledgements
The publishers appreciate the support of Faith Hall, Patrick Roe, Pat Jones, Marcus Wülfling and the Mercury Provident Society over this book.

British Library cataloguing in publication data
Cooper, Stephanie
The children's year: crafts and clothes for children and parents to make.
(Who's bringing them up?)
1. Handicraft – Juvenile literature
I. Title   II. Fynes-Clinton, Christine
III. Rowling, Marye   IV. Series
745.5   TT160

ISBN 1-869890-00-0   Hardback

ISBN 1-869890-10-8   Paperback

Published by Hawthorn Press,
Bankfield House, 13 Wallbridge, Stroud GL5 3JA
United Kingdom.
Copyright © 1986 Hawthorn Press.
Cover design and illustrations by Marye Rowling.
Typeset in Optima
by Glevum Graphics, 2 Honyatt Road, Gloucester.
Printed by Billing & Sons Ltd, Worcester

Contents

Introduction

Once we went on a summer camping trip with another family, having between us six children aged from eighteen months to seven years. In spite of having an entire beautiful Welsh field to ourselves (save a few sheep) the calm of the first evening was shattered by the discovery that our four-year-old daughter had neither her beloved pillow nor her doll to help her get to sleep. Both vital objects had been left behind in spite of lists and good intentions. She was inconsolable, and it was obvious that the need for something inanimate to cuddle must be met.

I borrowed a cheesecloth nappy (muslin diaper to some) from our store of them and began fashioning a 'tie' dolly, knotting the four corners for arms and legs and folding it over, stuffing a round head with bits of sheep's wool from the field and securing this with cotton thread. Dolly was born in time to be welcomed into open arms and taken to bed – much to the relief of us all.

The next day another child eyed the doll, asked to hold it, and – finger in mouth – "I wish I could have a dolly like that." Right! Out came another bit of cheesecloth and soon another little form emerged. We borrowed handkerchieves and dressed the dolls. The children found bits of wood to make chairs for them, acorn cups and tea-towel blankets. The dolls were a tremendous success, and interestingly enough continued to be loved by each child long after we had gone back home . . . when the camping trip became just a memory.

Such a tale is about improvising, but there are other factors in it too. Small children can be very pleased with simple things, and they sense the caring that goes into creating something for them. They can bring a wonderful imaginative world of their own to surround a simple toy. 'The Children's Year' is written by three mothers who have observed this in children, and indeed found for themselves and other adults what a pleasure it can be to make something by hand. Furthermore, they have definite reasons for doing so.

Stephanie Cooper, Christine Fynes-Clinton and Marye Rowling suggest that in the last hundred and fifty years we have been released from spending all our time in work that supports our existence. We are now freer to follow whatever path we might choose in life. But we may have lost something through this revolution. Advances in technology have meant that most of the objects with which we surround ourselves are factory made. A reaction to this was already happening at the end of the last century, when William Morris and his colleagues began the Arts and Crafts movement seeing the dangers of mass production in which the principles of cheapness and expendability overruled good design.

In the days before 'consumer society' a practical artistic sense could be passed on from adult to child. The child could watch crafts or handwork being practised and learn to recognise a thing of beauty made through the feeling and skill of the adult, before trying to make something for him or herself. The process of creating and the quality of real beauty are not commonplace today. When objects were made by hand, households must certainly have had fewer of them. In a strange way our age is one of poverty in quality rather than quantity. Whether we rely on jumble sales or enjoy high credit ratings, it is possible to surround our children with – possibly drown them in – things. The nature of things helps to form environments, and environments influence us and certainly influence the growing child. It is still possible for small children to enjoy floating leaves downstream or their own wooden construction in the bath without really needing a perfect replica boat. Soft dolls are warmer and more comforting to cuddle than finely-featured plastic ones. Older children take enormous satisfaction in constructive handwork with good materials. For many of us the actual activity and sense of purpose involved in making something is as important as the end result.

'The Children's Year' seeks to help in this realm. Here is a book which hopes to give the possibility to adults and childen alike to rediscover the joy and satisfaction of creating something that they know both look and feels good and can also be played with imaginatively. Like its predecessor 'Festivals, Family and Food', there is a seasonal basis for 'The Children's Year'.

We suggest that being in tune with nature's cycle and the rhythm of the year can help bring order and meaning to our households and personal lives. This is surely true for individuals of all ages, and the book is meant to have a wide appeal. Consider the following few examples of items to make.

Spring: 'Eye of God' symbol, Easter egg candles, child's rucksack, knitted ducks, chickens and rabbits, wooden somersaulting bear, felt flower fairies.

Summer: fabric print using leaves and flowers, oil lamps from oranges, mob caps and sunhats, rope ladder and tree walk, cup 'n' ball game, grass dolls.

Autumn: slippers and socks for all ages, knitted jumpers, woolly baby clothes, mittens, puppets, lanterns and gnomes, conker web, wooden rattles.

Winter: bird table, bird feeder, candle holders, wooden climbing gnomes, indoor 'camp', woven pencil case, Jacob's ladder and gift boxes.

This is a book for using, sharing and giving. It has clear instructions and abundant illustrations. May it help us – regardless of our ages – to know and actively keep alive the simplicity and wonder of the children's year.

Judith Large

General sewing instructions

The instructions in this book include a scaled down pattern marked out on squares representing 5cm (2") for each sewing project. To make up your pattern you will need some paper ruled up into 5cm (2") squares. You can make the squared paper yourself by ruling out the squares on a sheet of newspaper or wrapping paper, joining several pieces of paper together with sellotape if necessary. 5cm (2") squared pattern paper is also available from most haberdashery departments of large stores or from fabric shops. When drawing your pattern, mark the exact position of all the corner points shown on the reduced scale pattern in this book. Join up the points drawing the straight lines first and then joining them with any curved lines. Draw in the letter marks and mark the edge to be placed on the fold. Make dotted lines for the sewing line and solid ones for the cutting line. (1cm (³/8) seam allowance is shown and included on all patterns.)

Lay and pin the pattern pieces on your fabric. Great care is required when using 'one-way' fabric such as velvet or corduroy: All pieces of the garment must then run in one direction! For finishing and neatening edges there are three easy ways. Choose which suits you best:
a) If you have a sewing machine with a zigzag stitch, zigzag closely to the edge of the material.
b) If you have pinking shears, use them for cutting out. (This method is not very satisfactory when working with very thick materials that fray easily.)

c) Oversew all the raw edges by hand. This method is of course more time consuming but works well on all fabrics.

When you have chosen a project make sure you get everything prepared first, and as you proceed be sure that each stage has been completed correctly before you move on to the next. This will save a lot of frustration and heartache at the end, when you can look at the finished product and see that it is done well.

We wish you enjoyment and satisfaction in your work!

Knitting abbreviations

st(s)	Stitch(es)
K	knit
P	purl
st.st.	stocking stitch
g.st.	garter stitch
rep.	repeat
cont.	continue
sl.	slip
tog.	together
rds.	rounds
inc.	increase
dec.	decrease
psso	pass slip stitch over

The seasons corner or seasons table

Children like to have a special place to which they can bring their treasures. Here all the objects which they have found on walks and out playing can be shown off to advantage, rather than being left in pockets, under pillows or sadly lost too soon. It is especially important for those children who live in towns to keep them in touch with nature and the changing seasons.

Have the corner or table always in the same place with an area of free wall space behind where you can hang pictures. You can also hang things from the ceiling – for example, stars, birds and butterflies made out of paper. When the children bring in flowers, leaves, stones, shells etc. the corner will reflect the changing seasons. For the special festivals the corner can become a beautiful scene of celebration.

Easter:

After the bare branches of winter, new buds are beginning to appear. Your Easter tree with its decorated eggs hanging from its branches can stand in the seasons corner. Next to it, you can have an Easter garden in a bowl. This is made of moss with bulbs and the first flowers in it.

Whitsun:

Your Whitsun corner can be decorated with white doves, white and yellow flowers, and perhaps with a backdrop of white and yellow veils.

Midsummer:

At midsummer there is no shortage of lovely things to put in the seasons corner. Use flowers and grasses and make paper butterflies which you can hang up. If you have been to the seaside you can put stones and shells in a glass bowl if you have one, and fill it with water. They will gleam and glisten.

Harvest and Michaelmas:

You can make a little harvest festival with bunches of wheat, oats and barley. Add apples, nuts, grapes, rosehips etc. A lovely harvest loaf can complete the scene. Perhaps you have a picture of St Michael and the dragon, and this could be added as well.

Hallowe'en:

Pumpkin and turnip lanterns will look very inviting, glowing in the corner.

Advent:

When Advent comes you can prepare a garden made of moss which will have things added to it as the weeks go by, leading up to Christmas. In the first week of Advent the mineral world is found in the garden. You can put stones and crystal amongst the moss. In the second week the plants come to the garden. It is surprising what you can find outside even in winter. In the third week the animals come. You can put little wooden animals in the garden. Finally the human beings come and there are Mary, Joseph and Jesus and the shepherds. Behind the garden you can hang a blue cloth on which you can stick stars and moon.

Another idea is to have as many stars in the garden as there are days in Advent. The stars are laid in a path at the end of which is the empty stable. Mary (a crib figure) stands on the first star on the first day of Advent and she moves onto another star every day. The star that she stood on flies up onto the blue cloth behind. By the time it is Christmas, the sky is full of golden stars and Mary has arrived at the stable.

Spring

Now daisies pied, and violets blue,
And lady-smocks all silver white,
And cuckoo-buds of yellow hue
Do paint the meadows with delight,
The cuckoo now on every tree
Sings cuckoo, cuckoo.

Shakespeare

1
Rucksack

Any young child is proud to have his or her very own rucksack! The child can then pack up a favourite toy when going on a journey or even carry some of his own clothes and slippers. Children also love to help with carrying the shopping home. If the rucksack is used for going to school, it is a good idea to embroider the child's name on the front in a decorative way. As the rucksack has adjustable straps, it can be used for a 2 – 7 year old.

You will need:

60cm (24") material 90cm (36") wide (Denim or corduroy material are very suitable)
Matching thread
1m (39") bias binding 12mm (½") wide in a contrasting colour.

Eight eyelets
70cm (27½") cord (or two shoelaces) in the same colour as the bias binding
One D-ring (its straight side = 4cm (1½") long)
Four D-rings (their straight sides = 3cm (1⅛") long each.
Two buttons in the same colour as the bias binding

Instructions:

Make up the pattern (see p.175) and cut out all the pieces from the material. Neaten edges (see p.7).
Make up the two long and two short straps: With right sides together, pin and sew along the stitching line and turn each strap inside out. (The handle of a cooking spoon is a great help with this!) Fold each strap in such a way that the seam is in the centre, turn the ends in and oversew by hand.

Lay the back and front piece on top of each other with right sides together, matching the letters.
Slip two of the 3cm (1⅛") D-rings onto each of the short straps and fold the straps in half.

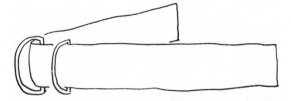

Now lay each folded strap in between the front and back pieces, 1cm (³⁄₈″) away from the side edges of back and front as shown.

Fold in and sew, towards the wrong side, a 2cm (¾″) hem across the front piece and side panels (e-c-d-e). Fixing the larger D-ring onto the back of the rucksack, fold in and sew the two side edges of the little square (S) towards the wrong side.

Fold up the lower edge of the square (S) 2cm (¾″). Slip the D-ring into this fold and tack the fold down. Fold the top edge 1cm (³⁄₈″) downwards and tack.

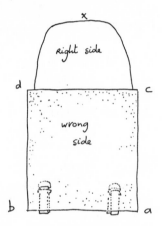

Pin and stitch twice along the bottom edge (a-b).

With right sides together pin and sew one side panel onto each side of the front piece, matching letters.

Pin and sew the square including the D-ring onto the right side of the back piece where indicated on the pattern.

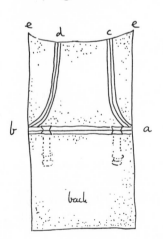

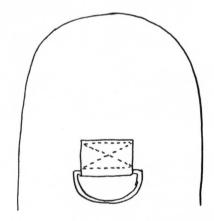

Put both long straps through the D-ring, (wrong side of straps on right side of back piece) and sew the ends down stitching along the folded edge twice.

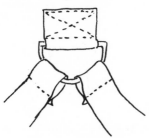

With wrong sides together, pin and sew along the side edges of the rucksack, matching letters a-e and b-e.
Important: These seams must be **5mm** (³/₁₆") away from the edge, not the usual 1cm (³/₈")! Bind the side seams and all around the top of the backpiece with bias binding. (Start at (a), going to e-x-e and ending at (b).)
Space out and put in the eyelets evenly around the hem e-c-d-e. (Follow directions on the eyelet kit as to how to put them in.)
Cut the cord in half and thread one through the eyelets at each side. Make a knot at each end of the cords to stop them from slipping out.

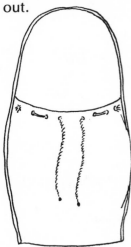

Make two buttonholes into the backpiece where shown on the pattern. Sew the buttons onto the corresponding places on the front piece. Adjust the straps to required length and fix them by threading them through the D-rings.

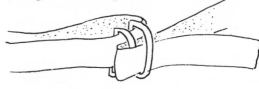

2
Somersaulting bear

This little, acrobatic bear tumbles head over heels along the bars. We usually think of teddy as somewhat lazy but look what he can do!

You will need:

Cardboard or plywood 30 x 13cm (12 x 15").
A sharp craft knife for the cardboard or a fretsaw for the plywood.
A hand drill.
A metal rod 14cm x 4mm (5½ x ⅛"). (If you cannot get hold of this you can use a 4" nail.

The width of the bars has to be reduced to 8cm in this case. See below.)
Glue (Uhu for the cardboard or wood glue for the plywood).
Paint
Greaseproof paper

Instructions:

Cut two strips – the top two bars – of cardboard (or plywood) 30 x 1½cm (12 x ⅝") each. Make a slot of ½cm (¼") at each end, 1½cm (⅝") from the end. These slots face downwards.
On the top side, make a notch as shown.

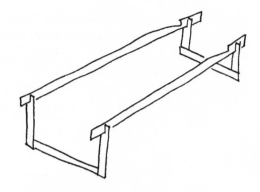

Trace the bear and transfer it onto the cardboard (or plywood). Cut it out.

30 cm (12")

Now you make the supporting frame.

Bars A and B are 9 x 1½cm (3½ x ⅝").
Bars C and F are 10 x 1½cm (4 x ⅝"). (These ones are only 8 x 1½cm (3¼ x ⅝") if you use a nail for the rod.)
Bars D and E are 6 x 1½cm (2½ x ⅝").

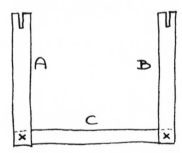

Make cuts at the top of bars A,B,D and E, again ½cm (¼") deep.
Glue these bars in place at the crossed points.
Assemble the whole.

Drill a hole through A, just large enough to hold the metal rod firmly.
Insert the metal rod until the bear is in the middle of it.
A bit of paint on the bear, carefully done, enhances the performance.

14

Now lay the metal rod across the bars at the highest point and the rumble-tumble bear is ready for performing. If you adjust the shape of the bear and it balances in any given position you can make the frame horizontal and it will run beautifully after a gentle push.

3
Balancing bird

What a lovely sight this bird can be rocking to and fro when you give it a gentle push! It looks distinctly exotic in its bright plumage of yellow, red and green with a dash of darker tones.

You will need:

Plywood or firm cardboard – 30 x 18cm (12 x 7")
Fret saw for the wood
or sharp scissors (or alternatively a craft knife) for the cardboard.
Paint, preferably yellow, red, green and ultramarine blue.

Watercolour or posterpaint
A straight stick ½ x 40cm (¼ x 16")
String 140cm (55")

Instructions:

Enlarge outline of the bird – see the back of the book. Trace it. Cut it out. Paint its feathers first on one side – let it dry. Paint the other side. A lot of the visual effect depends on the colours so give it a thought beforehand.
To make the perch make a small notch in the ends of the stick to prevent the string from slipping.

Tie on the string and hang it in a convenient place. Set your bird on it and give it a gentle push.

4
Cloth Basket

This is made like a clay coil pot. Using piping made for chair and sofa covers and cushions, you wind odd bits of material round it and coil it to make a little basket, sewing it together as you go. It can be finished off with a lid. If you have got bits of material which blend or match in colour, it will look more attractive.

You will need:

4.6m (5 yds) of piping (to make a basket 9cms (3½") in diameter and 6 cms (2¼") high).
Odd pieces of cloth
Needle and thread

Instructions:

Cut strips of material about 60cms (2ft) in length and 3cm (1¼") wide. Take a strip and wind it round the piping overlapping it as you go.

Also begin to coil the piping round in a spiral fairly tightly. Sew the coils firmly together. When the coil is 8cm (3¼") across, start building it upwards. Change the colours of material as you wish. When you have built up the coils to 6cm (2¼") cut off the piping and sew it down firmly.
Now make the lid with another flat coil and attach it on one side. You can sew a button to the side of the basket and attach a loop to the lid to keep it in place. With this method you could also make attractive table mats.

5
Cords

Lengths of cord are among the playthings that our children always need most. When they build camps they need cords to tie sticks and bits of cloth together. When playing horse or other animal games, they need the cords to be reins or leads. For dressing up they need belts. The edges of rivers and lakes can be indicated with a cord. Cords are quite easy to make – and cord-making in itself is a well-loved activity of many children. They can be made in many colours and with thick or thin wool, cotton or string.
Besides crocheting cords with a crochet hook, there are other ways of making them. Here are some:
see
1. Finger knitted cord
2. Twisted cord

Finger knitted cord

(Use thick wool for your first go.)
Make a slipknot in the middle of a long piece of wool. (A slipknot is the first stitch you put on the knitting needle when casting on stitches.)

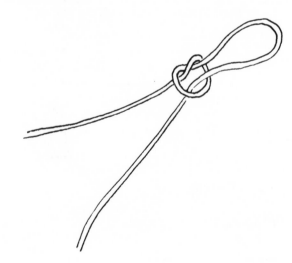

Put the loop over the index finger of your right hand. Hold the knot (below the loop) between your thumb and middle finger of your right hand.

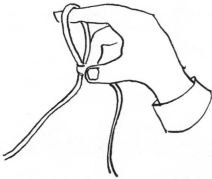

Put the index finger of your left hand through the loop and pull out a second loop, having the strand of wool on the left.

Move the knot which you are holding with your right hand over and hold it with the thumb and middle finger of your left hand.

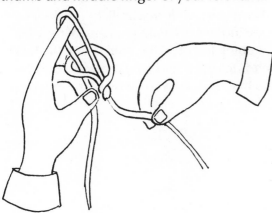

The right hand pulls its end of wool tight. Now put the index finger of your right hand through the second loop, have the wool on the right and pull out a third loop.

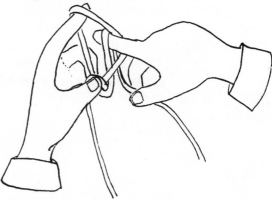

Let go of the knot which you are holding with your left hand and take hold of the knot with the thumb and middle finger of your right hand – your left hand pulls its end of wool tight. Continue to make loops over and over again using the left and right hand alternately.

Twisted cord

A twisted cord can be made in one or more colours.

You will need:

Two or more lengths of wool or cotton which are 2½ times as long as the length you want the finished cord to be. Find a stable object – doorknobs or a window latch – and tie one end of your length of wool onto this object. Hold the other ends in your hand and stand at a distance (far enough to make the strings taut between you and the doorknob or window latch).

When the cord begins to curl, take a pair of scissors and slip them along the cord into the middle.

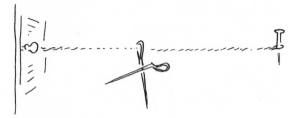

Make a knot to tie together the lengths of wool in your hand. Insert a pencil or a knitting needle into the end you are holding (see diag. 2) and keeping the strings taut, twist the knitting needle or pencil in one direction.

Ask a second person to hold the scissors in the middle while you walk to the doorknob or window latch with your end of the cord – keeping it taut all the time. Bring the two ends together and hold the cord up in the air so that the scissors can twist around freely.

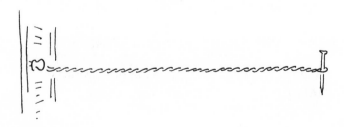

You will see the scissors spinning around for some time (stop them from turning in the opposite direction which they'll eventually try to do!). Take the scissors off and make a knot at each end of your beautiful, finished cord.

6
'Eye of God'

This comes from Mexico and is an Easter symbol. It is a most satisfying and decorative object to make and quite young children can be pleased with their creations. The secret of its effectiveness lies in the colour combinations that you choose. You can make single 'eyes' or more elaborate crosses with five 'eyes', one on each cross piece and one in the centre.

You will need:

Thin pieces of stick
Different coloured wools

Instructions:

For a single 'eye' take two sticks about 18cm (7") long. Choose the wool you want to use first and bind the end of it around the centre of the cross you have made with the sticks. By winding the wool round each crosspiece in a clockwise or anti-clockwise direction you build up a diamond shape which is flat on the front and shows the bound sticks on the back.

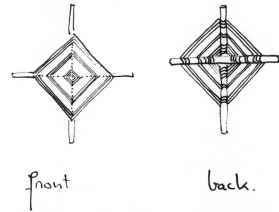

front   back.

If you are working from the front, you take the wool, say from the top cross piece down to the right cross piece, wind the wool once round from the front to the back, then down to the bottom cross piece and wind round from front to back etc. Change colour as you work outwards.

If you want to make a large cross, take two longer sticks and four shorter ones to make cross pieces on each end.

Make your central 'eye' larger than the four outer ones, and bind all the exposed stick that is left after you have made your five 'eyes' with matching wool. To finish it off you can add little tufts of wool to the end of each cross piece. It is now ready to hang on the wall.

7
Palm Sunday cross

Palm Sunday is the Sunday before Easter. On the continent children used to – some still do – walk with Palm Sunday crosses and sing songs. A Palm Sunday cross can change into an Easter cross on which one can hang the decorated Easter eggs.

You will need:

Bamboo, slats of wood or branches (4 pieces):
One 50cm (20") for the vertical, one 15cm (6"), one 22cm (9") and one 30cm (12").
String
Box (hedge) or some similar green. If this is not possible use green crepe.
Pink crêpe – 10cm (4") wide
Dough – for the cockerel on top
Raisins and small sweets
An orange
25cm (10") thin wire
Fresh small flowers

Instructions:

First make the cockerel. It requires as much dough as is needed for 2 buns. Model it into shape lying flat after the first rising. Make the neck and feet small, otherwise they might rise into one enormous blob. Put a currant in for the eye. Leave to rise and bake.

In the meantime make up the cross. Tie the three pieces 15-22-30cm firmly onto the vertical stick, and decorate these with the greenery. Put in fresh little flowers.
String up the raisins and sweets. Cut narrow strips of the pink crêpe. These can be tied onto the three branches. All this can flutter in the wind. An orange on the top cross bar signifies the sun. Fix it with the wire. The cockerel, when cool, goes onto the very top. You can decorate it still further with little spring flowers.

At the end of the day, or before, all the edibles get eaten and the flowers get removed. The empty cross can be put into a bowl with damp earth and cress or grass seed can be sprinkled onto it. It is remarkable how quickly these sprout, indoors.

Early on Easter morning, this cross can again be decorated with the blown and painted eggs and fresh flowers.

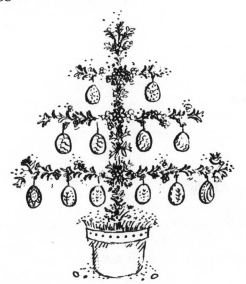

A beautiful variation is the middle cross in the second picture. Instead of the three horizontal sticks, you can use one bent into a circle. Tie the two ends together, and suspend it from the top with ribbons. Pale ones, yellow, pink or green – are in harmony with the season. Decorate as the other one.

8
A moving picture – ducks and fishes

If you dare to get out the watercolour paints and have a go at this pond with ducks and fishes, you will be surprised to see with how little you can make an exciting present; or let the children try it. They will enjoy bringing animation into their pictures.

You will need:

Watercolour paints plus brush
Firm watercolour paper about 30 x 25 cm (12 x 10") plus a little extra for the three loose animals.
Blue cardboard, a little larger than the painting paper and some offcuts for tabs. The blue should be the same as the water in the pond.
A paper fastener
Glue and scissors

Instructions:

Paint the picture. Paint only one duck and no fishes. Where the second (rocking) duck is going to be, just paint water. On the little extra piece of watercolour paper paint the second duck and two fishes in light orange. When these are dry cut them out. Stick the fishes onto a tab of blue cardboard.

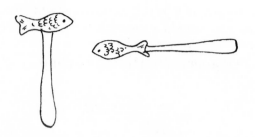

Make a slit in the water when the picture is dry and put the fish through it.

Make a slit in the form of a bulging wave. Put the paper fastener through the loose duck's tummy and put the duck's tummy behind the wave.

Put the picture in place onto the blue background and make a small hole with the split pin through the blue cardboard – fold the pin open. Now the duck is fixed and can rock. Glue the painted picture onto the blue background where it does not interfere with the fish and the rocking duck. The fish by moving the tabs, can swim to and fro on the water and the duck rocks on the waves.

9
A moving picture – an elephant

This large elephant's head moves at our command.

You will need:

Thin white cardboard approximately 25 x 14cm (10 x 5½")
Crayons
Two paper fasteners
Scissors

Instructions:

Cut the cardboard down from 25cm (10") to 18cm (7"). Put the strip aside.
On the main piece of cardboard draw your picture starting with the main theme which can be any animal with a neck but draw the head only very thinly in outline. Take the spare strip of cardboard and copy the headshape onto this with an extraordinarily long neck at least 6cm (2½"). Cut this out.

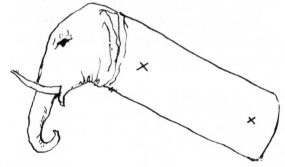

Finish the picture by colouring it all over and then colour the head.

Take a strip of spare cardboard 13 x 4cm (5 x 1½") and fold it double and glue it for strength. This is the pulling tab. Place the cut out head onto this tab and with the paper fastener through both pieces connect them at the end of the neck.

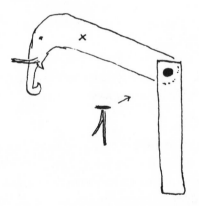

Make a slit in the main picture where the head is to be attached to the body. Make this slit in a curved shape, wider than the neck. Slip the head through it, into the right position. With another paper fastener through the body and neck, fix the two together.

By pulling the protruding tab, you move the animal's head.

10
Easter egg cosy

For your Easter breakfast table you can surprise your family with a colourful egg cosy to add to the Easter mood.

You will need:

Two pieces of 9 x 9cm (3½ x 3½") of golden yellow felt
Two pieces of 7 x 3cm (2 x 1") of pale yellow felt
Scrap pieces of bright red and orange felt
Yellow sewing cotton

Instructions:

Draw the shape of the chicken lightly with pencil, tightly fitting, on one golden yellow square. Cut two of these shapes.
Cut out a small beak in orange
Cut one comb in red
Cut three tail feathers: one feather in pale yellow, one feather in orange and one feather in red.
Cut two wings in pale yellow.

To make up the bird, turn the pencil line to the inside. Stitch the beak, comb, feathers and wings in their appropriate places. Pin and sew in blanket stitch with yellow cotton around the outside. Your cosy is ready for its egg.

How to blow eggs

This is a task for careful fingers!

Wash the eggs in water with a dash of vinegar in it. Dry them.

With a darning needle carefully bore a hole at each end of the egg, making the hole at one end slightly larger than the other. Break the yolk with the needle. Hold the egg over a bowl and blow through the larger hole until the egg runs into the bowl and the shell is empty.

actual size

Wash the egg again very carefully as a blown egg is fragile and cracks quite easily.

11
Egg decorations

Easter eggs are to be found in the garden, on the Easter tree or on the breakfast table. What fun to discover something so colourful amongst the new green leaves on this very special morning.

There are many ways to help the Easter hare with decorating eggs. A friend of ours knows 27 different ways! Here are a few. A practical hint: start well before Easter – some methods are not very quick.

First of all, try and find the palest eggs available. Some free range chickens still lay the old-fashioned white ones, but not many. The hunt starts here.

Tie-dyed eggs

You will need:

Either blown or raw eggs
Food dyes or lots of onion skins (The onion skins give a rich golden brown colour)
Small flowers and leaves
An old nylon stocking
Cotton thread

Instructions:

If you use raw eggs and food dyes, boil the eggs first. Do not boil them if you use onion skins. Cut a piece of stocking, just larger than the egg and tie up one end. Put the egg into it. Place the small flowers and leaves inside the stocking around the egg. Pull the stocking firmly over the covered egg – which is a little tricky – and firmly tie up the stocking on the other side.

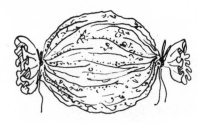

Dye this egg parcel in the food colouring. Mind that the colouring is not too strong,

otherwise the patterns will be lost. If you use onion skins, cover these with water and boil them up. If you use raw eggs make sure they are covered with the water and onion skins and boil it all together. The blown eggs can be boiled in it as well. It takes some time before the colour dyes the eggs strongly.

When done, take out the eggs, unwrap them and let them dry in an egg box. If you used blown eggs, let them dry out upside down with the small hole up. The delicate patterns of the flowers and leaves are printed onto the egg.

When it is fully dry, rub the egg with furniture wax polish to give it a sheen.

Dyed and painted eggs

This is a nice method to use with children who can use a small paint brush. Most of them from the age of 6 or 7 can do it.

You will need:

Pale, blown eggs
Food colouring – pale colour
Water colour
Very small paintbrush

Instructions:

Dye the eggs in a light overall colour and when dry, paint Easter motifs onto them.

These can be the traditional designs but your small artist will want to make his or her own! Suggest a hare, rising sun, small birds, little flowers, anything to do with the new Spring feeling. If you put the egg on a narrow knitting needle with some blu-tack above and underneath it to hold it in place, your chances of success will be increased!

Although felt pens usually in creative work give a harsh and flat effect, they can be very effective in drawing on eggs. They can be used instead of the paint.

Batik eggs

This is a very simple way of using the batik technique on eggs. Again you can do this with children from 6 – 7 years old onwards. For the advanced pychanhi technique you need all the proper batik tools which you can get from a craft shop. Instructions for this are included in the sets.

You will need:

Blown or hardboiled eggs

Candle
Batik dye or food colouring in 3 different colours (e.g. yellow/red/violet)
Paper tissues or toilet paper

Instructions:

Wash the eggs in water which has a dash of vinegar in it. Dry them carefully. Light the candle and with the melted wax drop a few drops evenly spread over the egg. Let them dry and dye the egg in a light colour (yellow). Again let it dry and drop some more wax onto the egg, now onto the coloured ground. Dye the egg again, now in a slightly darker colour (red). Repeat this process once more and dye the egg in the darkest colour (violet).

Let the egg dry again. When dry, hold it next to the candle flame (but not in it) and as the wax melts quickly wipe it off with the paper tissue. Repeat this till all the wax is removed. You will be surprised at the colour effects and at the sheen of the egg!

Scratched eggs

This method is not so easy but with some care older children can do it too.

You will need:

Pale hardboiled or blown eggs (the hardboiled eggs are firmer and do not crack so easily in this method which requires more force)

Food colouring or batik dye – dark colours only
A sharp knife or nail, ideal is a dentist drill bit (ask your dentist for old ones) held in a clutch pen
Black pencil and rubber

Instructions:

Dye the eggs. Dry them. They are now ready to have their patterns drawn into them. If you use blown eggs, remember that they are fragile, especially at the top and bottom. Hold the egg in the palm of your hand, avoid using just two fingers.

Use the sharp point of your tool and gently scratch away your drawing on the dye to reveal the white underneath. The traditional design divides the egg in halves horizontally. If you do not have a steady hand you can use a rubber band to guide you. Mark this line with a pencil and scratch this line away with your tool. Then divide the egg vertically. Do this again at right angles to your first vertical division.

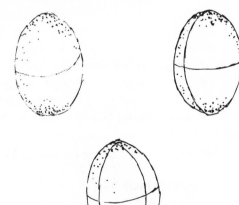

You now have eight parts. To finish the basic structure of the design, make a triangle in each part as shown.

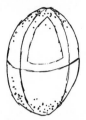

Now use your Easter imagination and design a figure in each triangle. First draw it and then gently scratch it out.

When it is done you can wax it with furniture wax polish to give it a sheen.

Some Easter egg motifs

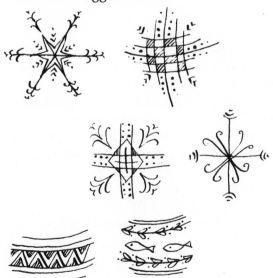

8cm (3") candlewick in narrow size
Some plasticine
Melted wax – enough to fill an egg

Instructions:

Carefully enlarge the hole at the bottom of the egg to about 2½cm (1") diameter. You can use nail scissors for this. Wash the egg, dry it, and with a small paintbrush oil the inside of the egg very thoroughly.

Melt the wax in a container that stands in boiling water. Add colouring if you like. Dip the whole wick in hot wax and pull it straight while it is still soft. Thread the wick through both holes in the egg. Seal the small hole by putting some plasticine around the wick. Line an eggcup with aluminium foil and stand the egg in it (large hole on top). Slowly pour some wax ino the egg, holding the wick in the middle. Slowly fill the egg with wax to the top. Keep the wick in place with two matches as you let the wax set for about 15 minutes.
After 15 minutes, check to see if a well has appeared around the wick. Break the surface skin of the wax with a skewer and top up with more hot wax around the wick.

12
Easter candles

The candles in the shape of an egg are fun to make. It is a great moment when you can crack the eggshell and find a new egg inside the cracked one!

You can make the candles from candlewax that is available in most craft shops or from old candles that are melted down. To colour the candle we either used some wax dye or little bits of broken wax crayon. We have seen some very charming candle-eggs which had been made in a light colour and were decorated with little transfers of spring flowers.

You will need: (for one candle)

1 blown egg
A little oil

This topping up process may need to be repeated, as wax shrinks when it cools down. When the candle has finally cooled and set (after a few hours or overnight), crack the eggshell and remove it. Trim the wick and level the base of the candle.

You can decorate the candle with transfers or by glueing small, pressed flowers all around the sides.

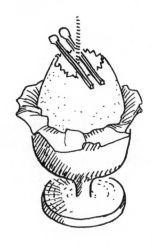

13
A pop-up Easter egg card

Little children love moving pictures. The pop-up Easter egg card they can make themselves.

You will need:

Three pieces of light coloured card 14 x 20 cm (5½ x 8")
Coloured pencils, crayons or paint
Scissors and glue

Instructions:

Cut out two pieces of card A and B in the shape of an egg, approximately 14 x 20 cm (5½ x 8"). Cut a round window 5 cm (2") across in A just above the centre. Cut a piece of card C a little bigger than the window with a tab long enough to protrude below the lower edge of A when it is in position behind the window.

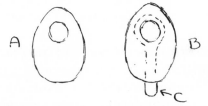

With C between them stick A and B together along the edges, except where the tab C sticks out. The popup Easter egg is now ready for the pictures to be added. Seasonal images are a jumping hare, a rising sun or Easter flowers.

14
Duck and ducklings

This is a pattern that children can easily make as the duck is made of two squares only. Children who have just learned to knit will enjoy making ducks like this as they do not take too long.

You will need:

20gr (1oz) yellow double knitting wool
1 pair no. 3mm (2US) knitting needles
Some fleece for stuffing
A scrap of orange felt for the beak
Brown or blue thread for embroidering the eyes

Instructions:

For the body cast on 20sts and knit 48 rows. Cast off.
For the head cast on 10sts and knit 24 rows. Cast off.
Fold the bodypiece in half (the knitting rows running horizontally). Sew the top edges together.

Run a thread through the edge at one end and pull together.

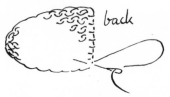

Stuff the body and sew up the back starting at the top. Draw the last stitch into the body and secure. This is a way of 'modelling' the shape of the duck.

back

Fold the headpiece in the same way as shown for the bodypiece and sew together as shown. Draw one end together in the same way as the front of the body.

Stuff the head and sew up the other side using the drawing together method.

Sew the head onto the body in the appropriate place. Cut out a beak from the orange felt in the shape as shown.

Fold the beak in half and sew it onto the front of the head. Embroider the eyes onto the sides of the head.

For a little duckling's body, cast on 10sts and knit 24 rows. For its head, cast on 5sts and knit 12 rows. Finish by following the instructions given for the big duck but making the beak much smaller.

15
Knitted Easter chicken

A whole family of chicks on a patch of green moss is a lovely addition to your Easter table. This is a very simple knitting pattern which can be made by children.

You will need:

3mm (3US) knitting needles
A small amount of yellow wool (4 ply)
A scrap of orange felt
Some fleece or cotton wool for filling
A bit of blue embroidery thread

Instructions:

With your yellow wool cast on 3sts. Knit 1 row. On the next and every alternate row increase one st. at each end. When you have 20sts on your needle knit one row. On the next and every alternate row decrease one st. at each end until only 3sts are left. Cast off. Fold the square in half Y to X.

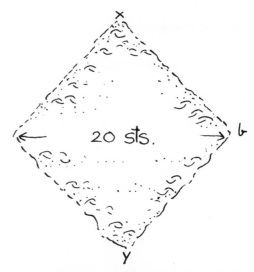

Sew up one open side of the triangle XYB and put in the filling. Sew up the other side of the triangle. Pull the top corner slightly inwards to make a more rounded shape which will form the head. With a few stitches around the neck shape the head.

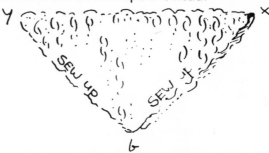

Cut the orange felt like this for the beak and sew the beak with small stitches to the head.

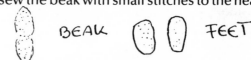

A stitch with the blue embroidery thread on each side of the head will make the eyes. Cut two feet from the orange felt in the given shape and sew them to the bottom so that the chick can stand on its own.

16
Chicken and cockerel

Here is an opportunity to knit a whole farmyard set; the chickens and cockerel are quick and simple to make.

You will need: (for the chicken)

A small amount of white or brown double knitting wool
One pair 3¾mm (4 US) knitting needles
A small amount of red and yellow wool for comb, wattle and beak
One 3mm (C US) crochet hook
Some fleece or cottonwool for stuffing
One white button

Instructions:

Cast on 18sts and work in garter stitch.
K 3 rows.
In the fourth and every following row K the first 2 sts together. Continue until there are 6 sts left. Cast off.
Fold this triangular piece in half and sew up one side.

Stuff this triangle and sew up the other side.

With the red wool, crochet the chicken's comb by making three sts into the same place. Embroider beak with yellow wool and wattle with red wool.

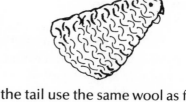

For the tail use the same wool as for the body. Crochet four rings with 4-5 chain sts each.

Sew on the button with hollow side facing downwards to make the chicken stand.

You will need: (for the cockerel)

A small amount of white or brown double knitting wool
One pair 3¾mm (4 US) knitting needles
A small amount of red, green and yellow wool (or embroidery cotton)
One 3mm (C US) crochet hook
Some fleece or cotton wool for stuffing
One red button 1½ – 2cm (⅝ x ¾") diameter

Instructions:

Knit and make up the cockerel exactly in the same way as described for the chicken. The only difference is in the tail:

17
Easter egg wheel

A variation on the Easter egg card is the Easter egg wheel.

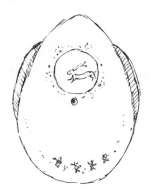

You will need:

One piece of light coloured card 14 x 20cm (5½ x 8″)
One round piece of card 16cm (6¼″) diameter.
One paper fastener (see picture)
Pencils, crayons or paint
Scissors

Instructions:

Cut out one shape of an egg approximately 14 x 20cm (5½ x 8″). This is A.
Cut a window in A, 5cm (2″) across, just above the centre.

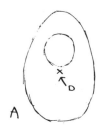

Cut the circle B, 16cm (6¼″) in diameter. With a pin through the centre of circle B

locate D underneath the window in such a way that the circle always covers the window when the wheel is turned. Mark through the window onto the circle B, the top and bottom of the window. Turn the wheel and locate in this way the band which will be visible through the window. Take it apart and make your picture series on the band always with D in the middle and the picture on top – a bounding Easter hare, birds, Spring flowers and a rising sun, can be your theme.

Then decorate the front. This could be done in one colour with flowers around the outside. Finally, with the help of the paper fastener, assemble the two pieces through D and the wheel is ready for turning.

18
Easter rabbit

This is a woolly Easter rabbit which small children can make too. It is made from woolly balls in three different sizes.

You will need:

A small amount of brown wool
A tiny bit of white wool
A scrap of brown felt to make two ears
Card for the woolly balls
Thread

Instructions:

Follow the instructions for making woolly balls in the mobile on p.138. Make one ball 5cm (2") in diameter. This is the body. Make a smaller one for the head. Make a tiny white one for the tail. Sew all three together as shown in the drawing. Cut out two ears and attach to the head.

19
Easter tree

At Christmas we decorate a fir tree. For Easter, the branches of trees which are just about to produce leaves or flowers can be made beautiful. Birch and/or forsythia look very nice. From these branches hang the blown and decorated eggs.

You can put these branches either into a large vase, or in a large flowerpot filled with earth. If you like, you can moisten the earth and sow some seeds in it; mustard, cress or grass. If you do this a week before Easter, these seeds will have sprouted.

To suspend the blown and decorated eggs, you need matches and cotton thread. Break a match in half and tie some cotton firmly onto it. Push this, with one point down,

through the larger hole and pull it gently back up. It will lodge itself into the egg.

Make a loop at the top of the cotton and you can suspend the egg.

20
Easter garden

Fill a flat dish with pebbles and moss. Put halved egg shells amongst them which are cleaned out and filled with earth. Sow seed in them – wheat, millet, cress or marigolds. In between the shells you can put chicks or the Easter hare.

Prepare all this well over a week before Easter, so that you can see the new shoots on Easter morning.

21
A willow whistle

Spring is the best time to make willow whistles as it is then easiest to remove the bark from the wood without tearing it. You can find willows on damp ground and near streams.

You will need:

A straight piece of willow, without knots, 10cm (8") long and 1½cm (¾") wide.
A sharp pocket knife

Instructions:

Cut away the mouthpiece
Cut away a piece for the air flow.

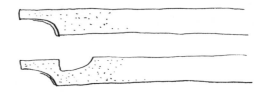

Cut a band of 1cm (½") of bark only 10cm (4") away from the top.

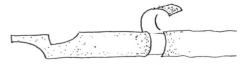

With the back of the knife, tap the bark gently for about two minutes.

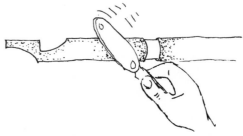

Very carefully turn and twist the bark off the white wood. It must not tear.

Cut 1 to 2mm (less than ⅛") away from the white wood top of the mouthpiece.

Cut the white wood away between the dotted lines.

Put the inside of the mouthpiece back in the bark – and insert the bottom piece.

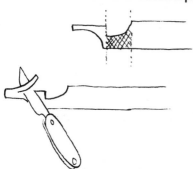

The willow whistle is now ready. When you blow and change the position of the bottom piece you can vary the tone and even make a simple tune!

Two hints: keep the whistle in a damp cloth – if it dries out it is useless: and if you want to stay friends with your family, try the musical bit out in the open air!

22
Spring flower fairies

During the bleak days of February when we are waiting for the first signs of Spring, we can anticipate the flowers by making little flower fairies out of felt. This is something to do with children as it calls for only simple stitching. The snowdrop is followed by the crocus and celandine, then come primroses and violets in March.

Snowdrop

You will need:

White felt 12.5cm (5") square
Green felt 12.5 x 7cm (5 x 2¾")

One pipe cleaner
One 2cm (¾") diameter bead for head
Glue and thread

Instructions:

Fold the pipe cleaner in half, push the folded end through the bead and fold over 1cm (⅜") to stop the bead slipping off. Secure with glue.

Cut a strip of white felt 7 x 12.5cm (2¾ x 5") for the dress. Sew the short sides together using an overstitch. Gather the neck edge and pull tight around the pipe cleaner and tie round the neck.

To make the hat, cut a piece of white felt 8 x 4cm (3 x 1½") and shape the petals.

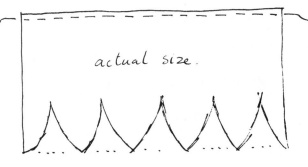

actual size.

Sew as for the skirt and gather tightly round the green felt stalk. The stalk is made from a circle of green felt about the size of a penny.

green.

Make the leaves from a piece of the green felt 12.5 x 5cm (5 x 2").

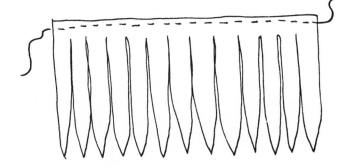

Gather the top edge with green thread and join together round the neck over the dress. Glue the hat onto the bead.

Crocus

You will need:

Purple felt 12.5cm (5") square
Green felt 12.5 x 5cm (5 x 2")
Scraps of golden yellow felt
One pipe cleaner
One 2cm (¾") diameter bead for head
Glue and thread

Follow the instructions given for the snowdrop. Make dress and hat from purple felt. To show the characteristic golden yellow colour of the stamen cut a scrap of golden yellow felt as shown on Diagram 5. Gather the hat tightly round the yellow stamen as shown on Diagram 5A.

5

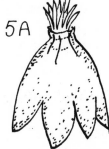

5A

The leaves are the same as the ones for the snowdrop.

Primrose

You will need:

Light yellow felt 12.5cm (5") square
Green felt 12.5 x 5cm (5 x 2")
One pipe cleaner
One 2cm (¾") diameter bead for head
Glue and thread

Follow the instructions given for the snowdrop. Make the dress and hat from light yellow felt. To make the hat cut an 8 x 4cm (3 x 1½") piece of light yellow felt as shown.

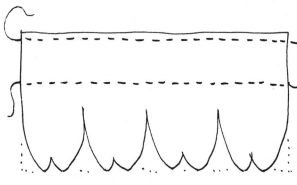

Gather tightly at the top of the hat and run through another thread in running stitch. Gather 1cm (⅜") below the top of the hat as shown.

Follow the diagram for cutting the leaves from your green felt and secure over the dress as described for the snowdrop.

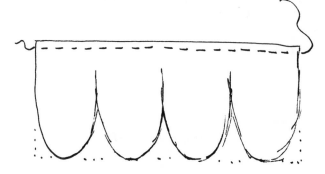

Violet

You will need:

Dark violet felt 12.5cm (5") square
Green felt 12.5 x 5cm (5 x 2")
One pipe cleaner
One 2cm (¾") diameter bead for head
Glue and thread

Follow the instructions given for the snowdrop. Make the dress and hat from dark violet felt. Cut and sew the hat as shown in Diagram 9 and Diagram 10.

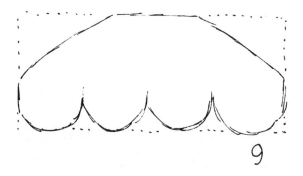

9

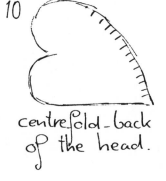

10

centrefold - back of the head.

Cut leaves from green felt as shown in Diagram11 and secure over the dress as described for the snowdrop.

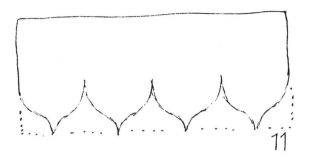

11

23
Silk rainbow fairy mobile

This mobile makes a lovely present for a baby who will like watching the softly coloured fairies floating and dancing over his or her cot. The mobile will move beautifully if it is hung near a window or radiator.

You will need:

A piece of very light-weight white silk (at least 12.5 x 63 cm (5 x 25")
Watercolours (pastel shades)
Small quantity of cotton wool (or sheepswool)
About 50 cm (20") of centre cane (No. 8)
Transparent nylon thread

Instructions:

Wash the silk to get rid of the sizing so that it will take up the colours more readily. While it is still wet, stretch it out on a flat surface (a piece of white melamine board is ideal). Mix the watercolours and test colours on a spare piece of material. Paint the colours in over-lapping bands starting with yellow-orange, pink, blue, then yellow again. By over-lapping the colours you will get the rainbow hues appearing, for example the blue on the pink will make lilac.

Leave silk to dry on the board, then iron it and cut into squares 12.5 cm (5"). Roll little balls of wool, about the size of a marble and place in the centre of the silk square. Wrap around neck with thread and tie securely. Make five fairies.

Thread a needle with a 20 cm (8") length of transparent thread and make a double knot at one end.

Push the needle through the underside of the head, drawing out at the top of the head. Cut three lengths of cane 25 cm (10"), 10 cm (4") and 13 cm (5"). Tie the fairies to the cane as shown. Secure each thread on the canes with a dab of glue when you have balanced the mobile.

Alternatively try this rainbow.

24
Paper boxes

These boxes have many uses and can be folded to make any size. They make very nice presents if you put a little treasure in them – some sea shells, a polished stone, beads, some pretty ribbons or little biscuits or sweets. In the olden days chemists used the rectangular box to weigh out medicine powder.

The rectangular box can be made from a postcard, and will be strong enough to hold nails, pins or drawing pins. You could even make a tiny pillow and blanket and use the box as a bed for a doll's house.

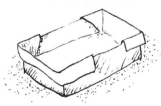

The square box can be made with a lid by using a slightly bigger box to fit over a smaller one. The lid can be decorated with cut out paper shapes – a heart for Valentine's day, a star for Christmas, a hare for Easter or some flowers for a birthday or Mother's Day.

You will need:

Some strong card (plain or coloured)

Instructions:

Rectangular Box

Fold the postcard in half lengthwise to find the centre and open flat again. Fold each long outside edge in to the centre crease, and open flat again. You should now have three parallel fold marks.

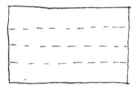

Turn the paper sideways and repeat to locate the folds running at right angles to those you have already made. Leave the edges folded into the middle.

Fold corners to meet dotted lines.

Fold out centre edges over corner folds as shown. Pull up at points marked * and the box will take shape.

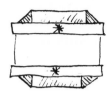

Square Box

If you use a piece of paper measuring 20 x 20cm (8 x 8") you will get a box 7cm (2") square.
Fold the square diagonally in half.

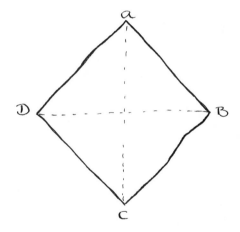

Bring the corners a, b, c, d to centre point X.

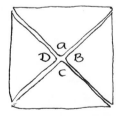

You now have a much smaller folded square of paper. Open all the folds.

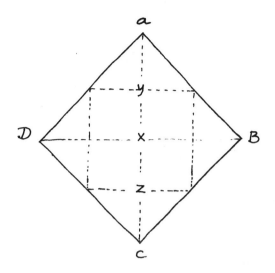

Make more folding lines by folding c to y and after opening the square up again, fold c to z.

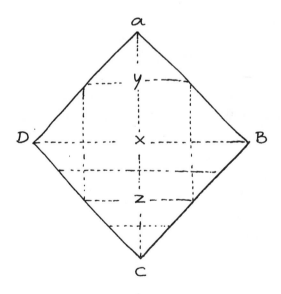

Repeat the same procedure on each side with corners a, b and c.

41

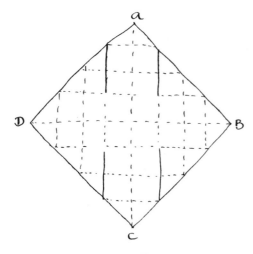

If you want a lid for your box, make it in exactly the same way but start with a square that is 1cm (³/₈″) bigger than the one which you used for the base box. You can make the box into a kind of basket by fixing a strip of paper to the sides of the box.

Cut along the lines which are shown as solid lines. Fold corners d and b into the centre and make the sides of box as shown.

25
The plank

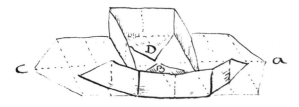

Now fold the two sides with corners a and c in such a way that they meet in the centre of the box.

In our household, the plank has been for years the most simple and at the same time the most versatile play thing around the house and garden. It can be played with by itself as a slide, or see-saw, or it can be used as a link between two climbing obstacles.

We saw it often between a climbing frame and a work bench.

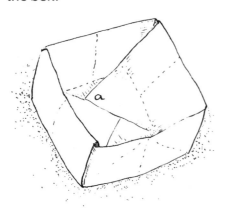

It can be part of a building, part of a roof with veils or sheets covering it. It makes an ideal companion to the 'camp'.

And when the children are past building their play houses, the plank can be used as a bench for sitting on or as a shelf.

You will need:

The wood (our plank is 2m x 23 x 2cm (7ft x 9 x ¾"))
Rasp
Sandpaper, medium and fine
Four small strips of wood 18 x 4 x 2cm (7 x 2 x ¾")
Eight screws and woodglue
Linseed oil and old rags for putting it on

Instructions:

The plank needs to be sanded down very well: nothing is more offputting than a splinter from a toy!
First use the rasp, then use the medium sandpaper. Finally use the fine sandpaper, until the wood feels like silk. Sand both top and bottom and round off the edges.

Place the four little strips of wood in place: see drawing. Glue and screw these. The two outside strips are there to prevent the slide from falling off a ridge. One of our worktops has an identical strip, so that the two quickly and safely steady the slide.
The two middle strips steady the seesaw when it lies across a tree trunk or bottom ridge of a sturdy fence.

Finally, many thin layers of linseed oil make it shiny and weatherproof.

26
Caterpillar bookmark

This is a little present that a child can make in a short time.

You will need:

A scrap of double knitting wool
A 3.5mm crochet hook
Two very small glass eyes or black beads
Glue or thread for fixing eyes

Instructions:

Crochet a length of chain (using chain stitch) as long as you want your bookmark to be. A good average length is 23cm (9″). Turn at the end of the chain and, starting into the 2nd stitch from the hook, work 4 trebles into one chainstitch.
Repeat this about 10 times. You will find that the crochet stitches will twist around the chain and your caterpillar will emerge! Sew in the thread and glue on the glass eyes or sew on the beads in the appropriate places (see drawing).

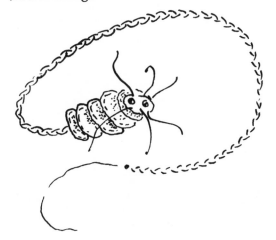

If you want to make a 'hairy' animal, thread short lengths of wool through the face of the caterpillar, knot them and cut them off.

(Another suggestion is to make one caterpillar at each end of a chain and use them for tying around a girl's pony tail!)

Summer

When the green woods laugh with the voice
of joy,
And the dimpling stream runs laughing by;
When the air does laugh with our merry wit,
And the green hill laughs with the noise of it;

When the meadows laugh with lively green,
And the grasshopper laughs in the merry
scene;
When Mary, and Susan, and Emily
With their sweet round mouths sing, "Ha,
ha, he!"

When the painted birds laugh in the shade,
When our table with cherries and nuts is
spread:
Come live, and be merry, and join with me,
To sing the sweet chorus of "Ha, ha, he!"

Laughing Song: William Blake

27
The rope ladder and tree walk

A rope ladder can be made by older boys and girls for their secret tree camps, or just to get into an awkward tree.

You will need:

Twice the length of rope you want the ladder to be, plus some extra for knots.
Strong pieces of wood 3cm (1¼") diameter, each to be cut, 30cm (12") for the rungs.

Instructions:

On both sides of the rungs make incisions as indicated.

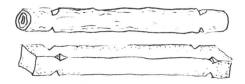

Tie the two ropes together at the top and suspend from a low branch. Open up the rope and insert the rung.

Make a knot just under the rung. Repeat this with the second rope at the same level. This is your top rung. Tie some string firmly above the rung and below it to prevent the wood from slipping. Repeat this so that you can space your rungs comfortably.

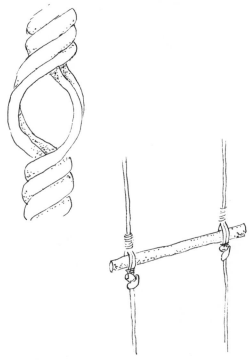

Finish by tying a knot in each of the two bottom ends of the ropes, to prevent them from fraying. Then position your ladder but make sure your knotting is safe.

If you have two trees not too far apart and rope (i.e. sash) for twice the distance and a bit extra, you can make a treewalk by tying the rope very securely from one tree to the other and back again, 1m (40") higher. Do not do it high up to start with because it takes some practice to walk on it, as you will find out!

28
Hip horse

As a variation on the hobby horse this is great fun.

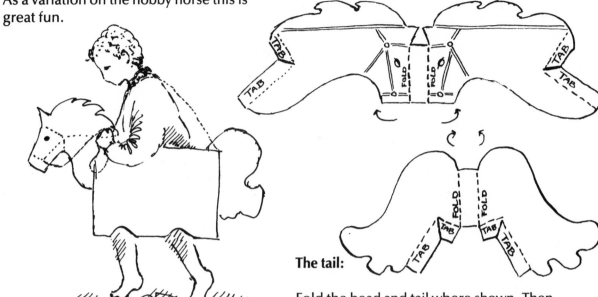

You will need:

One cardboard box 30 x 40 x 30cms high
1 sq.m. of cardboard (40 x 40")
276cm lightweight rope or clothes line
Paints
Wool for mane and tail
Odd bits of material for decorating

Instructions:

Take the cardboard box and cut the flaps off the top. Turn it upside down and cut out a piece of the bottom that goes right across the box and leaves 10cm at each end. This hole should be big enough to fit over your child's head and shoulders. Then cut away a scallop on each side of the box to suggest the horse's belly and legs. From the square cardboard you cut out the horse's head and tail. Using up half the cardboard for the head, the other half for the tail.

The tail:

Fold the head and tail where shown. Then fold the tabs and sew or staple them to the cardboard box, head at one end and tail at the other.

Now your horse is ready to be decorated. Draw a saddle shape on each side of the box and around the hole. Paint your horse with some thick paint, tempera or acrylic, whatever colour you want. Paint the saddle, mane, tail and eyes. You can paint on the bridle if you do not want to use ribbon. The mane and tail can have wool added to make them really flowing.

When it is ready the horse must now have reins and shoulder straps. Punch a hole through the lower ring of the bridle and insert a length of light rope or ribbon. Pull it through the ring on the other side of the nose, so that there is equal length on both sides. Pull it over the horse's head and tie the ends together.

To make the shoulder straps use similar material and find the right length by measuring your child from shoulder to waist. Make a hole on either side of the horse's head, and either side of its tail. Push the two ends of each shoulder strap through the holes and knot firmly. Your horse is now ready to gallop away.

29
Bean bag frog

He likes to be thrown from one person to another, or from one hand to the other, or he just sits on a shelf with his legs dangling down.

You will need:

A piece of material 40 x 22 cm (15¾ x 8½")
Two beads for the eyes
Some kind of dried beans for the stuffing; about 7 oz (185 gr) will be enough.

Instructions:

Draw round the outline on p.176. Cut it out. Pin the pattern to the material which you have folded to make double thicknesses, and cut round it. Remove the pattern and place the right sides of the material together. Tack the two pieces together leaving a 1 cm seam, going almost right round the frog but leaving enough room to get the stuffing in. Now machine it, turn it inside out and when you have put the stuffing in, finish it off by hand.

Sew the two beads onto the head for eyes.

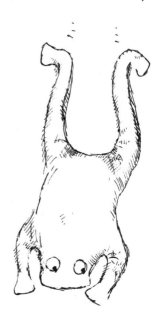

30
Harness

This is a lovely toy for two. Who will be the horse and who will be the rider? It is important that it has bells on it that will jingle. You can embellish it as you want with braid, felt decorations etc.

You will need:

¾ metre (29½") of cotton denim or similar
weight cotton
Two bells
Four press studs
Trimmings – braid, felt etc.

Instructions:

Cut out two layers for the main piece of the
harness. The harness is 75cm (29½") long,
13cm (5") high at each end, and 21cm (8¼")
at the highest point in the front.

Put the wrong sides of the material together
and machine nearly all the way round with a
1cm (⅜") seam, leaving a hole where you
can pull the harness inside out, but also
leaving two spaces 5cm (2") wide on the 'bib'
where one end of the shoulder straps will be
attached. Also, leave two spaces 5cm (2")
wide, 10cm (4") from each end of the
harness where the other end of the shoulder
straps will be sewn.

Cut two pieces 30 x 12cm (11¾ x 4¾"). Fold
them in half longways with the wrong side of
the material outside, and machine a 1cm
(⅜") seam. These are the shoulder straps.
Pull the right sides out, and sew them onto
the harness. Sew on the two bells at the top
of the bib where the shoulder straps are

attached. For the reins, cut a strip 7cm (2¾")
wide and 1½ metres (5') long. Fold in 1cm
(⅜") on each side and machine along.
Attach the reins to each end of the harness.
Sew on four press studs on the ends of the
harness. Add decorations to your liking and
the horse can now gallop away.

31
Whitsun dove mobile

It is a very special surprise for children to
find this mobile of doves spiralling down to
earth on Whitsunday! Hanging over the
breakfast table, the slightest draught or the
heat of a candle flame makes them move
softly.

You will need:

One 20cm (8") diameter wooden ring
(usually used for Macramé, available in craft
shops)
A piece of white card or strong paper about
22 x 18cm (8½ x 7")
One sheet of white tissue paper
Some white thread (if available, use gold or
silver thread)

Instructions:

From the white paper or card cut out a dove
as shown.

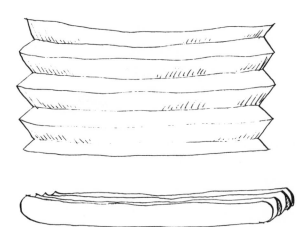

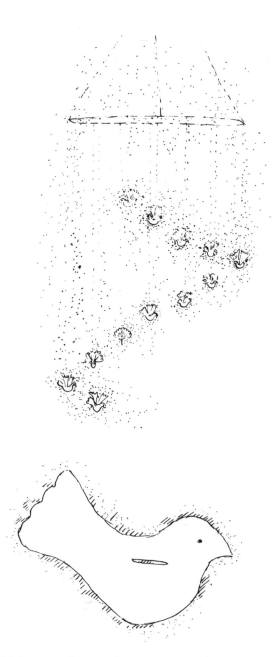

Insert the folded tissue paper through the slot in the body piece and open it up in a fan-like way. Now pull up the wings so that they meet in the middle and join them together by carefully threading a length of cotton through each side.

The dove can now be hung up on that thread. Make eleven more doves!
It is easiest to hang the ring up before fixing the doves onto it.

With some fine nail scissors or a sharp craft knife cut a slot for the wings where indicated. Cut a piece 10 x 8cm (4 x 3⅛) from the tissue paper, fold and trim the corners as shown.

To achieve the 'spiralling' effect, the first dove needs to be tied to the ring so that it hangs 5cm (2") below the ring. The thread of each following dove needs to be about 4cm (1½") longer. (The second dove hangs 9cm (3½") below the ring, the third dove 13cm (5⅛") below the ring etc.)
Space the doves out evenly around the ring.

32
Flying ricebags! and streamers!

Fun for outdoors! Twirl this little bag fast round and round. Let go and see it fly through the sky, so high, sometimes too high...

Instructions:

Place the ends of the three strips of crêpe paper and the end of the string onto one side of one square of cotton.
Place the other square on top and sew through the crêpe, string and cotton, around three and a half sides, leaving enough space to turn the bag inside out.
Do this and fill with rice or beans.
Sew up the opening and have fun flying!

You will need:

Two scrap pieces of cotton in a nice colour, each 10 x 10cm (4 x 4")
Rice or beans
A piece of string 70cm (28")
Three brightly coloured strips of crêpe paper 4 x 150cm (1½ x 60")

A variation on this are the streamers

You will need:

Three crêpe paper strips of 4 x 150cm (1½ x 60")
60cm (23½") dowelling
Glue

Instructions:

Glue the crêpe ribbons onto the top of the dowelling. When it is dry you can twirl it around, make circles, figures of eight, even write your name in the air!

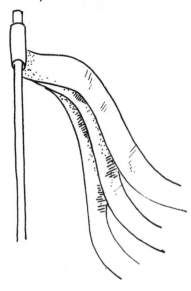

33
Butterflies

These butterflies make a lovely mobile if several of them are tied to a branch. Tied to the end of a stick they make a nice toy for a child to run along with.

You will need:

Pipe cleaners
Tissue paper in several (at least two) different colours
Sewing thread for hanging them up

Instructions:

Take two different colours of tissue paper and cut a square 10 x 10cm (4 x 4″) out of each.

Place the paper squares on top of each other and fold in half. Cut round the edges into the shape of a butterfly's wing.

Fold a pipe cleaner in half and twist the folded end slightly to form the tail. Slide the tissue paper wings between the pipe cleaner, pushing them towards the tail end to give a ruffled effect.

Twist the pipe cleaner at the head end leaving the ends to form feelers.

Tie a thread to its back so you can hang it up.

34
Garlands

A simple plait made of straw, raffia or dried grasses and knotted together at the ends makes an easy base for a garland which can be used over and over again. In Spring and Summer you can use fresh flowers and leaves or dried ones in the Autumn. Once the flowers wilt you can just pull them out and remake it when you need it again. They make good 'crowns' for a birthday child or to wear at Summer festivals.

Use 90cm (36") lengths of straw or raffia for the plait. Bind the ends together with a single strand to start with and secure the ends of the plait with the same strand when the plait is long enough. Don't make the plait too tight otherwise the flowers may be difficult to push in.

May garlands can be produced quickly by making a circlet of goosegrass and sticking buttercups and daisies into it. This can be a good game for a birthday party.

Tie the knot according to the size of the head.

35
Cup 'n' ball

Your children can easily make this paper cup themselves. It can be used for a traditional game of cup 'n' ball and also for a drinking beaker if the paper used is strong enough.

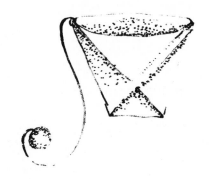

You will need:

A piece of paper 20cm (8") square
Some string
A wooden bead about 2cm (¾") in diameter

Instructions:

Fold your square of paper in half diagonally.

Fold both corners across as shown.

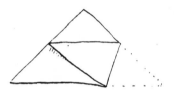

Now fold down the triangles at the top, one at the front and the other at the back.

Open the cup and tie your string to one of the corners by threading the string through a needle and pushing it through the paper. Fix the bead at the end of the string with a knot on each side to prevent it slipping.

36
Grass doll and grass horse
Small grass table mat, basket and heart

When the grasses are still young, but already high, these grass figures are fun to make and could be part of a summer table.

Grass doll

You will need:

Approximately sixty blades of pliable green grass about 50cm (20") long
Strong green wool

Instructions:

Soak the grass for about one hour.
Shake off excess water. Line up the grass heads and bend the grass as shown. Trim the blades so that they are just as long as the grass heads. Insert the arms (which are the cut off blades). Trim. Tie as shown. For an exotic hairstyle you can insert some grass heads.

Grass horse

You will need:

Three bundles of grass (about 10 blades in each) of equal thickness and length
Strong green wool, closely matching the colour of the grass

Instructions:

Soak the grass for about one hour.
Shake off the excess water.
Bend and tie the first bundle as indicated.

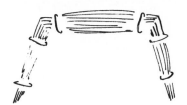

Repeat this with the second bundle.
Together these are the four legs and part of the body. Trim appropriately.
Bend the third bundle as shown to make up the head, neck and body. Tie firmly.

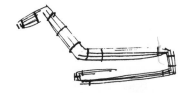

Assemble the three parts.

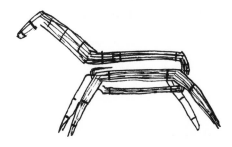

For the mane and tail you can insert a few grass heads.

Small grass table mat, basket and heart

This is not a project for those suffering from hayfever. But everyone else will enjoy making these grassy items out of nature's abundance.

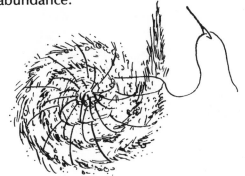

You will need:

A big bundle of pliable, long green grass
Strong green wool
Large embroidery needle

Instructions:

Soak the grass blades for about one hour and shake off the excess water. It is easiest to work on a large table.
Make a long grass bundle about 1.5m (60")
by layering the grass heads and then tying them. The bundle should be about 2cm (¾") thick.

Roll up the beginning of this bundle; this is the centre of the circle. With a needle and strong wool sew it as shown in the first picture. Make it as large as you want it and cut off the excess length in a layered manner as shown. If you keep it flat, it is a table mat, if you work the sides up it turns into a basket or a bird's nest, but do not make it larger than 12cm (5") as it becomes weak.

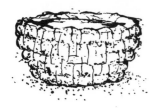

From a leftover you can make a decorative heart. Fold the grass in half. This corner is the bottom point. Turn the two sides towards each other and bend the insides a bit further as shown.
Simply tie a red ribbon as indicated to hold the halves together.

**37
Flowerpot bells**

You can create an interesting musical instrument if you make several of these flowerpot bells in different sizes. They can be hung in a row from a low branch of a tree or from a broomstick that is lying horizontally over the back of two chairs. Just one bell could hang by the door which your visitors could ring when they come!

You will need: (for one bell)

A clay flowerpot which is not cracked
(Big pots will make the bell ring with a deep sound. The smaller the pot, the higher the sound.)
Two wooden beads. (They must be larger than the hole in the base of the pot.)
A piece of strong string or a shoelace which is about three times as long as your pot is high

Instructions:

Thread one of the beads on one end of the string and make a knot to stop the bead from slipping off. Now measure the height of your flowerpot and make another knot to secure the second bead about 2½ cm (1") shorter than the height measurement of the pot.

Thread the string through the hole at the base of the flowerpot so that both beads are inside. The bell can now be rung.

Make a loop with the rest of the string so that you can hang up your bell. See diagram 2. If the hole in the bead is large enough to take a double thickness of string make the loop as shown.

Variation:

Use a longer bit of string and one additional bead so that the bell can be rung from below.

Your instrument:

Only use one bead for each bell:

With a spoon you can hit the bells and play a tune.

38
Play veils

This is one of the simplest pieces of play equipment but one which has the greatest scope for using the imagination. If you have different coloured veils, they can be used for dressing up or for camps, shops or castles, or for games with other play things such as bricks and animals where they become fields, sand, seas and rivers etc. A prince or princess can be created very quickly with a veil and perhaps a crown made out of foil or even coloured paper folded over a few times and fixed with glue or a paper clip.

You will need:

Pieces of gauze 92cm (1yd) square
Red, blue and yellow dyes
From these you can make purple, green and orange dyes as well

Instructions:

Dye the material according to the instructions on the dyes, and hem all round the edges of the material.

39
Baby's felt ball

This is a lovely present for a baby. Soft to hold, made with pretty colours and with a jingling bell hidden in the middle. It is made out of twelve pentagrams which together make a dodecahedron.

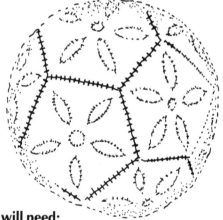

You will need:

A piece of coloured felt 36cm (14") square
Small pieces of different coloured felt but colours which go nicely together and match the background
Cotton thread

Small amount of wool fleece for stuffing
One small bell
Cardboard 8 x 8cm (3 x 3")

Instructions:

Cut a template having traced the diagram, out of a piece of cardboard. From this cut twelve pentagrams. You then have to cut five petals and a centre for each flower that will be sewn onto the twelve pentagrams.

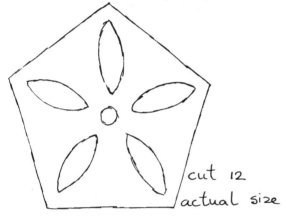

cut 12
actual size

Sew five petals and a centre onto each pentagram. Then sew the pentagrams neatly together, leaving the final one open so that you can push the stuffing and the bell in. Stuff the ball quite firmly or it will lose its shape. Finish sewing it up and your ball is ready.

40
Gnome in the shell

This charming little toy is excellent to take on long journeys. Small children love to watch the little gnome hiding in the shell and then peeping out again and again...It is a little fiddly to make, but well worth it!

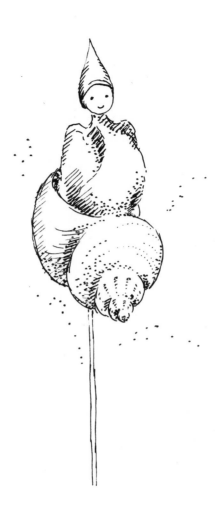

You will need:

One large whelk shell
One plain wooden bead 2mm (15/32")
diameter
One thin stick 14cm (5½") long (3mm basket cane is ideal)
One piece of thin cotton or silk material 10 x 13cm (4 x 5")
Matching thread
Some strong glue

Instructions:

Make a small hole in the bottom of the shell (just big enough for the stick to pass through). For best results scratch the place where you want the hole to be with a sharp needle and then use a small handdrill.

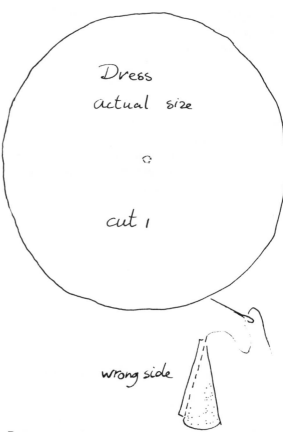

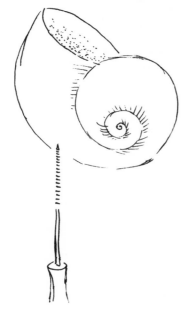

From the material cut out the dress and hat of gnome.

Sew up the back of the hat on the wrong side.

Put a spot of glue on one end of the stick and fold the circle of materials over the stick so that the glue touches the centre of the wrong side of the material. Tie a bit of thread tightly around the top of the stick to secure material in place.

Glue the bead onto the same end of the stick over the material. Turn the hat the right side out and glue onto the bead. Draw a tiny face onto the bead if you wish to. Put the stick through the hole in the shell and glue the bottom of the dress onto the inside of the shell.

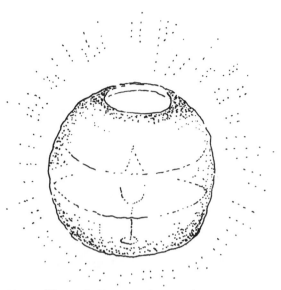

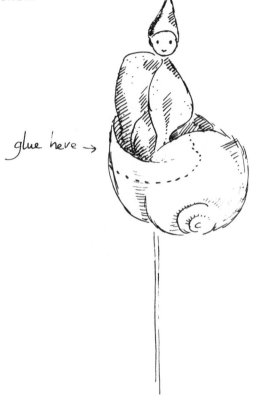

glue here →

You will need: (for one lantern)

One thick skinned orange
5cm (2") narrow candlewick
One drawing pin
Sunflower oil or other vegetable cooking oil

Instructions:

Cut the orange horizontally in half. Scoop out the flesh with a spoon. (Take care not to damage the skin.) Cut an opening 2½cm (1") in diameter in the middle of one half – this will be the lid.

**41
Orange oil lamp**

These little lanterns look very pretty in groups of two or three. They make nice garden lights for a summer evening party. Choose oranges that stand well without rolling over!

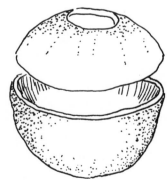

Tie the wick around the drawing pin.

Put the drawing pin with wick into the centre of the bottom half of the orange and half fill with the oil. Your lantern is now ready to be lit. When burning, place the lid on top of the bottom half.

42
Fabric printing with summer leaves

This is a way of turning quite plain things like pillowcases, napkins, tablecloths or bags into very special gifts. Although it needs care it is an activity in which school children can easily join.

Use a fabric paint which will not wash out. Use fresh leaves (dried or limp leaves will not work) such as Strawberry, Dandelion, Birch, Bracken. Vine leaves are especially suitable. Shiny leaves like Holly or Ivy are not absorbent enough and do not work.

You will need:

Fabric paint
Fresh leaves
Cotton or linen material
A small painting brush
Some newspapers and kitchen roll and other sheets of paper

Instructions:

Unless you have had plenty of practice it is best to print your fabric before making it up. Have a trial run with some scraps of material first. Make up a palette on a saucer with the paints. Choose your leaf and lay it right side up on a newspaper. Using the paint brush coat the leaf with one or more colours. With great care pick up the leaf and place it paint side down on the fabric. Cover the leaf with a sheet of kitchen roll to soak up any excess paint.

With another sheet of paper (not newspaper) on top of this, press down with your fist to make the image. Iron your print on the wrong side of the material to fix the colour (following paint instructions on jar). Only print one leaf at a time if you are making a border pattern. Iron when the border is complete.

You will need:

1.4m (1½yds) material 90cm (36″) wide
1.24m (4ft 1″) elastic 10mm (⅜″) wide
Matching thread

short version.

43
Baby's jumpsuit (9-18 months old)

This jumpsuit is very practical, especially once the baby starts crawling about. It is easy to make and easy to wear with plenty of room for nappies! Make it from cotton material (seersucker and cotton velour are especially nice for this project). The jumpsuit can also be made in a short version for use in hot weather.

Instructions:

Prepare the pattern (see p.177) and cut out both pieces from the material. For the straps cut out four pieces, each measuring 30 x 5cm (12 x 2″).
Neaten the edges on the trouser pieces. With right sides together, sew centre front seam (x-a). Sew centre back seam (y-b) leaving a gap of 3cm (1¼″) from top. Clip the curves and press the seams open. Match centre front and centre back seams and sew the inside leg seam. (From the bottom of one leg across the crutch and down to the bottom of the other leg.)

Clip the curves and press the seams open. Turn top edge 5cm (2″) to wrong side and press.
To make the casing for the elastic:
Topstitch three seams, 1cm (⅜″), 2.5cm (1″) and 4cm (1⅝″) from the fold at the upper edge.

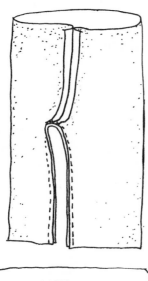

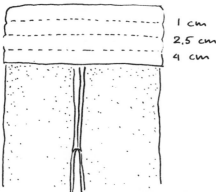

1 cm
2.5 cm
4 cm

To make up straps: Fold the strap pieces lengthwise in half (wrong sides are folded together). Fold both long edges 1cm (³⁄₈") towards the inside and stitch these edges together, turning in the edges at one end.

Pin and tack each strap to the inside of the top edge, 8cm (3¹⁄₈") on either side of the centre back and centre front seam. Topstitch the straps in place exactly on the stitching lines which run along 1cm (³⁄₈") and 2.5cm (1") from the upper edge.

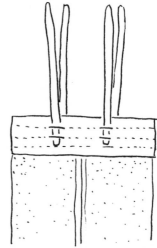

Cut two 48cm (19") lengths of elastic and run one length through each casing. Overlap ends of elastic and sew together securely. Turn the ends of the legs up 1cm (³⁄₈") and then 3.5cm (1³⁄₈") on the inside and press. Topstitch two seams 2cm (¾") and 3.5cm (1³⁄₈") from the fold at the bottom of each leg, leaving a gap in the upper seam through which the elastic is inserted. Cut two 48cm (19") lengths of elastic and run one length through each casing. Overlap ends of elastic and sew together securely.

44
Dungarees/pinafore

These are nice and roomy play dungarees, which are easy to make as there are no zips or buttonholes to tackle. They can be made in needlecord, or thin velvet for the winter and in thinner cotton material for the summer. The legs can be shortened and you will have a sun-suit. The pinafore version is even faster to make! If the material is plain the bib can be embroidered or trimmed with some braid or lace. Use your imagination...

You will need:

Material which is 90cm (36") wide:
2.4m (2²⁄₃yd) for 8-9 year size
1.8m (2yd) for 4-5 year size
1.6m (1¾yd) for 2-3 year size
Matching thread
44cm (17¼") elastic 10mm (³⁄₈") wide

Important:

As there are three sizes drawn in one pattern, the stitching lines are not indicated. The seam allowance is 1cm (³⁄₈") as usual.

Instructions:

Prepare and make up the pattern (see p.178). Cut out all the pieces from the material, plus 4 pieces 30 x 5cm (12 x 2") each for the straps. Neaten all the edges of the trouser pieces. Take the trouser fronts and with right sides together sew centre front seam (a-b). Clip the curve and press seam open. Take trouser backs and repeat with centre back seam (c-d). With right sides together match front and back trousers and sew the side seams from x to the bottom. Press seams open. Topstitch around the openings x-y.

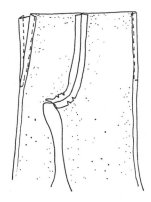

With right sides together, taking care to match centre front and centre back seams, sew the inside leg seam. (From the bottom of one leg across the crutch and down to the bottom of the other leg.)

65

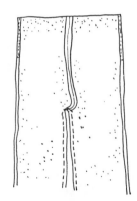

Run two rows of gathering stitches along the top of the front and the back of the dungarees.

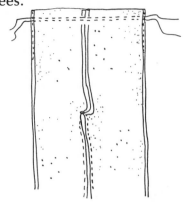

To make up each strap: On the wrong side fold both edges 1cm (³/₈″) lengthwise towards the middle of the strap. Fold the strap in half, lengthwise again and sew along the edge, turning in the edges at one end.

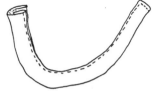

With the right sides together, pin the two bib pieces on top of each other. Insert one strap on each side between the two bib pieces and sew around the edge.

Turn the bib with straps the right way out. Repeat to make the other bib. Draw up gathering stitches to fit the length of the bib. With right sides together, pin one layer of the bib to the gathered front of the dungarees. Tack and sew.

Press the seam towards the bib. On the unsewn layer of the bib, turn in 1cm (³/₈″) hem and slip stitch the edge to the previous sewing line on the bib.

Turn the ends of the legs up 1cm (³/₈″) twice on the inside and press. Sew the hem leaving a gap through which the elastic is inserted. Having cut the length of elastic in half, pull one piece through the hem. Adjust the elastic to fit round the child's ankle. Overlap and stitch securely. Close the gap in the hem through which the elastic was inserted.

Pinafore variation:

Make up the bib and straps as in dungarees pattern. To make the skirt, cut 2 pieces of material 56cm (22″) wide by the length of dress required, adding 4.5cm for a hem.

With right sides together, sew side seams leaving a 10cm (4") gap at the top edge for the armhole opening. Press seams and topstitch around the armhole opening as described for the dungarees. Gather and sew to the bib as shown for the dungarees. Turn up the hem.

45
Hairband

These hairbands can be made in many different colours. Older children can make them for their friends choosing different motifs for decorating each one. Such hairbands also make ideal birthday party gifts.

You will need:

A band of felt about 40cm (15¾") long and 2.5cm (1") wide
Scraps of felt in a contrasting colour
A bit of elastic 2cm (¾") wide x 10cm (4") long
Thread and glue

Instructions:

Decide on the motif you would like to use for decorating the hairband.

Make a motif pattern on a piece of paper, cut it out and lay your pattern on top of the contrasting coloured felt. Draw around the edge of the pattern with a pencil and cut out your design in felt. You will need about eight hearts, stars or flowers. With a dab of glue put the motifs in position on the hairband spacing them out evenly. With thread in a matching colour, stitch each motif onto the band using a small running stitch.

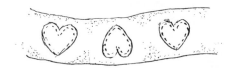

Round off the corners at both ends of the hairband. Sew the elastic onto the inside at both ends of the band, forming a circle.

Variation:

For a much quicker result, use a length of nice braid instead of the felt!

46
Baby's sunbonnet

It is as important to protect a baby's head from the hot summer sun as it is to keep warm in winter.

The size given is for a baby of about 5 – 10 months.

You will need:

50cm (½yd) of 90cm (36") wide cotton fabric (Broderie Anglaise is very suitable)
45cm (17¾") Broderie Anglaise lace edging (This is gathered when purchased)
60cm (24") of 1cm (⅜") wide satin ribbon
One small button in matching colour
Matching thread
Strong thread or embroidery cotton in matching colour for loops

Instructions:

Prepare the pattern (see p.179) and cut out all the pieces of the hat from the cotton material. With right sides together, pin and sew around the edge of the bonnet (starting at a, ending at e), leaving the front of the bonnet (a – e) open. Trim close to the stitch line, clip the curves and clip into corners.

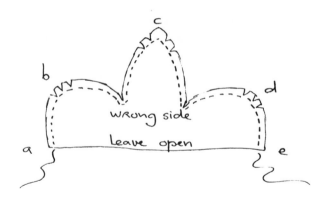

Turn the hat right side out. Press. With some strong thread make a loop large enough to fit around the button on each side where indicated at b and d. Sew around the loop using buttonhole stitch.

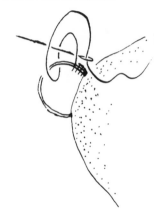

Sew the button on to the bonnet where indicated at c. You can now button up the bonnet.

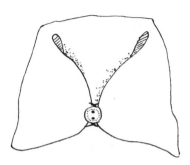

To make the brim, baste the bound edge of the lace edging along the seamline around the outside edge of one brim piece.

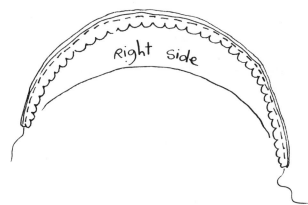

With right sides together pin and sew the two brim pieces together along the outer edge. (The lace edging is now between the two brim pieces.) Trim close to the stitch line and clip the curves. Turn the brim right side out. Press. On the outside of the bonnet, with right sides together, pin and sew the brim to the hat matching centre marks X.

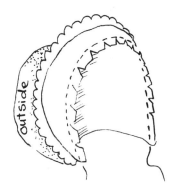

Trim the seam and press both seam and brim towards the hat. Turn the whole bonnet inside out and pin the inside of the bonnet over the brim seam turning the edge under. Slipstitch in place.

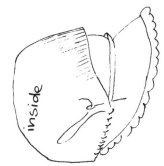

Cut the ribbon for the tie ends in half and sew one ribbon onto each side of the bonnet at points a and e.

47
Mob cap

This is a very good way to make a sunhat which could be matched with a dress. It also could be made as a hat for a dressing-up box as it does not take much time to make and is very effective even when made out of an old bit of sheeting. The size given will fit a 2 – 10 year old!

You will need:

One square of cotton material 44cm x 44cm (17½" x 17½")
2.5m (2yds 36") bias binding (in a contrasting colour if wished)
45cm (18") of 6mm (¼") wide elastic band

Instructions

Cut the material into a circle with a diameter of 44cm (17½").
On the wrong side, draw another circle 6cm (2½") inside the first circle, using a pencil or tailor's chalk.

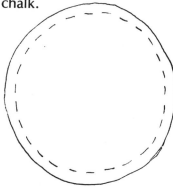

Centre the bias binding onto the second circle. This is the casing for the elastic. Pin and stitch, folding the ends under.

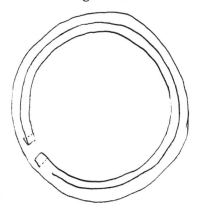

Bind the outer edge with bias binding. Pull elastic through the casing, overlap the ends by 1cm (⅜") and stitch together securely.

48
Toddler's sunhat

This sunhat will protect your toddler's head from the sun in summer. It looks nice on a girl or boy.

The size given is for a child of about 18 months to 3 years.

You will need:

50cm (½yd) of 90cm (36") wide cotton material
25cm (¼yd) of 80cm (32") wide medium weight interfacing
Matching thread

Instructions:

Prepare the pattern (see p.180) and cut out all the pieces of the sunhat from the cotton material. Cut out the brim piece from the interfacing. To make the crown of the hat, pin and sew the four hat panels in pairs with right sides together.

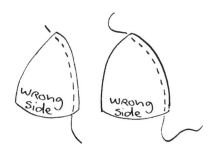

Press the seams open and clip the curves.
With right sides together pin and tack the
two crown sections together in one
continuous seam.

Neaten the seams.
To make the brim, iron the interfacing to the
wrong side of one hat brim piece. With right
sides together pin and stitch the centre back
seams of both brim pieces. Trim the
interfacing close to the seam. Press seams
open. With right sides together pin and tack
the two brim pieces together and then stitch
close to the outer edge.

Trim close to the stitchline. Turn the brim
right side out. Press. With right sides
together, pin and tack the top side of the
brim and interfacing to the crown. Sew and
trim.

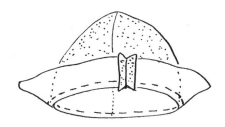

Now pin the bottom side of the brim to the
crown and handstitch in place.

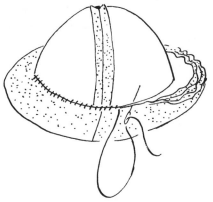

To finish the hat, topstitch four lines right
around the brim starting near the outer
edge. Keep the lines 1cm (³⁄₈″) apart.

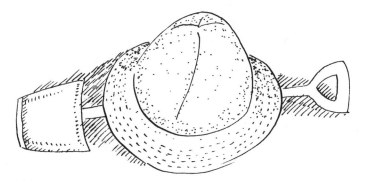

49
Baby's bonnet

This bonnet is very practical as well as
charming because it really covers the baby's

ears! For a winter baby, it is knitted in wool and for a summer baby, in thin cotton or silk. The size given is for about 6 to 12 months. (For a smaller size use No. 3mm (3 US) knitting needles.)

You will need:

30gr (1oz) 4 ply wool or cotton
One pair size 4mm (6 US) knitting needles

Instructions:

For the frill, cast on 160 sts and knit 8 rows in g.st.
Next row: K2 tog. and repeat this until the end of the row. You now have 80 sts left.
Carry on knitting in st.st. until work measures 12½cm (5") including the frill. On next right side row start to decrease:
1st row: *sl 1, k 1, psso, k 8*. Repeat from * to * to the end of the row (72 sts left).
2nd and every alternate row: Purl.
3rd row: *sl 1, k 1, psso, k 7*. Repeat from * to * to the end of the row.
5th row: *sl 1, k 1 psso, k 5*. Repeat from * to * to the end of the row.
7th row: *sl 1, k 1, psso, k 5*. Repeat from * to * to the end of the row.
9th row: *sl 1, k 1, psso, k 4*. Repeat from * to * to the end of the row.

11th row: *sl 1, k 1, psso, k 3*. Repeat from * to * to the end of the row.
13th row: *sl 1, k 1, psso, k 2*. Repeat from * to * to the end of the row.
15th row: *sl 1, k 1, psso, k 1*. Repeat from * to * to the end of the row.
17th row: *sl 1, k 1, psso*. Repeat from * to * to the end of the row.
You now have 8 sts left.

Break the thread and gather the 8 sts on a needle and pull the thread through the stitches. Your 8 sts will now form a neat little star at the back of the bonnet. Sew the back seams together over the 9cm (3½").

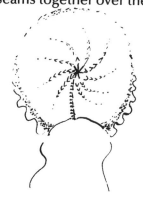

As the cotton yarn tends to stretch a bit when the bonnet is in use, you might find it necessary to weave a length of elastic thread through the front of the bonnet just behind the frill. This stops the bonnet from slipping off too easily.
Crochet two strings measuring about 25cm (10") each and sew one on each side of the bonnet just behind the frill.

50
Toddler's popover apron

This is a very practical little apron with a

72

crossover back. As there are no buttons or ties it easily slips over the head. It will fit from about 18 months to 2½ years.

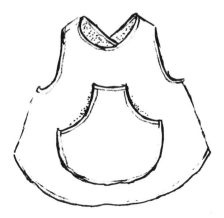

You will need:

64cm (25") cotton fabric 90cm (36") wide
3.45m (11ft 4") biasbinding in a contrasting colour
Thread

Instructions:

The pattern (see p.188) shows a 1.3cm (⅝") seam allowance at C and A-B. All other edges are bound with the bias binding. Neaten edges A-B and C as preferred (see general instructions).
Bind the edge of the pocket all the way round with bias binding starting at D. Pin the pocket into position on the front of the apron and topstitch, leaving D-E open on both sides. Join sideseams A-B with right sides together. With wrong sides facing, cross the two backsections and join shoulder seams C as shown in the diagram. Bind the edge with one continuous piece of bias binding starting under one arm at A.

51
Smocks

These smocks do not only look very nice but they have also proved to be very useful. They can be worn as blouses in summer and over thick woollies in winter. It is much easier to wash and dry a cotton smock than a thick jumper!
Add to the length of the smock and you will have a little girl's dress. Use some brushed cotton to make a nightie.

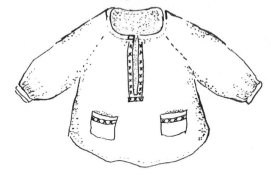

Smock for a 3-4 year old

This smock has long raglan sleeves which are gathered with some elastic round the cuffs. Use some braid to decorate the pockets and around the front opening.

You will need:

1.10m (43½") cotton fabric 90cm (36") wide
70cm (27½") braid (about 1cm (⅜") wide)
Matching thread
One small button
38cm (15") elastic, 5mm (³⁄₁₆") wide

Instructions:

Prepare the pattern (see p.181) and cut out all the pieces from the material. Neaten all edges (see p.7). With right sides together, pin and sew up the centre front seam, matching letters (g-o). Press seam open. To prepare the pockets, turn in and press all four edges of each pocket (1cm, ⅜") on the wrong side. Baste.

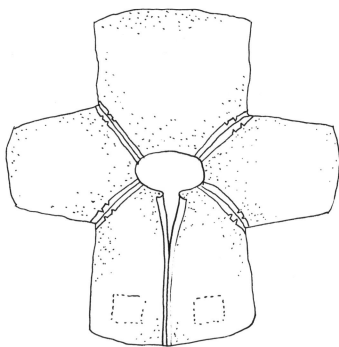

Turn the pockets onto the right sides and pin and stitch a length of braid across their front edge, folding ends under. (At the same time stitching down the top hem.)

Pin the pockets on the fronts where indicated on the pattern and topstitch three sides close to the edges. Pin the sleeves to the armhole edges of front and back, right sides together, matching letters b-d and c-f, stitch. Clip curves. Press the seams open.

Pin and sew the neckband to the neckedge, right sides together, matching letters n at centre back. Press the overlapping ends of the neckband at centre fronts onto the wrong side. The turned in edges of the neckband and front pieces must be in a straight line.

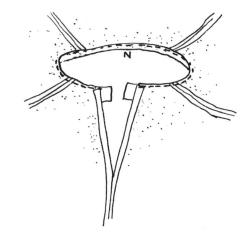

Press the free edge of the neckband 1cm (³⁄₈″) onto the wrong side and pin in place along the stitching line. Hemstitch by hand.

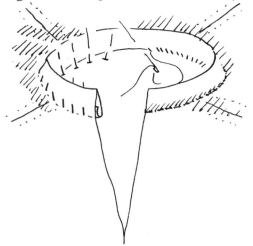

With right sides together, pin and stitch underarm and side seams of the sleeves and smock, matching raglan seams. Clip the curves and press the seams open.

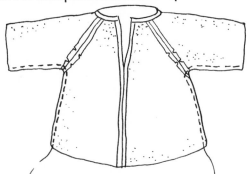

Turn in and stitch the sleeve hems, leaving a small gap for threading the elastic through.

Cut the length of elastic in half and thread one piece through the hem on each sleeve. Sew the ends together securely. Turn in and stitch the hem all round the bottom edge of the smock. Pin and topstitch the braid around the front opening. Sew the button onto one end of the neckband and make a loop on the other side.

Sleeveless smock for a 1 - 3 year old

This is a lovely smock with decorative shoulder pieces. The straight neckband doubles as casing for the cord. Use some braid to decorate the shoulder pieces and around the front opening. This smock is especially suitable for making into a dress by adding to the length of back and front!

You will need:

60cm (24″) cotton material 90cm (36″) wide
80cm (31½″) braid (about 12mm (½″) wide)
Matching thread
70cm (27½″) cord to tie around neck

Instructions:

Prepare the pattern (see p.182) and cut out all the pieces from the material. Neaten all the edges (see p.7).
With right sides together, pin and sew up

centre front seam, matching letters (f-o).
Press seam open.
Make a row of gathering stitches 1cm (³⁄₈") below the stitching line on each shoulder seam, (b-c and d-e) where indicated on the pattern.

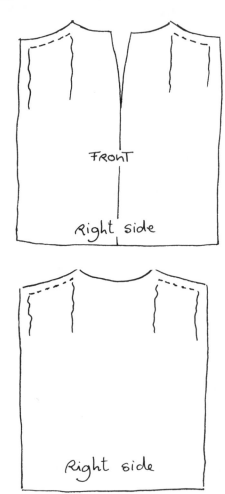

Place the shoulder pieces on each side of the neck with the wrong side of the shoulder piece on the right side of the smock, matching in with the shoulder seam line. Pull gathering threads so that the neck and armhole edges of the shoulder pieces are in line with the neck and armhole edges of the smock. On the right side, top stitch the shoulder pieces onto the smock.

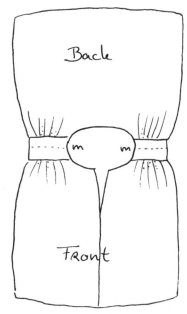

Pin and stitch the shoulder seams of back and front, with right sides together (b on e and c on d). On the wrong side of each shoulder piece, turn in and baste sides e-d and b-c on the stitching line.

Pin and sew neckband casing to neck edge, right sides together, matching letters x at centre back. Press overlapping ends of the neckband at centre fronts onto the wrong side, so that the edges of the neckband and the front edges are in a straight line.

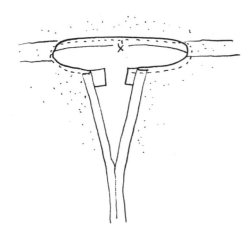

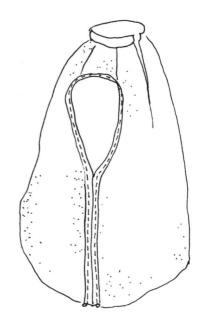

Press the free edge of the neckband 1cm (³/₈") onto the wrong side and pin in place along the stitching line to form a casing around the neck through which the cord will be threaded. Hemstitch by hand.

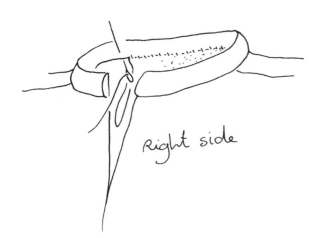

Right side

Turn up and sew the hem around the bottom edge of the smock. Pin and topstitch the braid onto the smock.

Thread the cord through the neckband casing. Make a knot at each end of the cord to stop it from slipping out.

With right sides together, sew up the side seams on each side of the smock (z-y). Fold in and pin the edge of these seams, starting at the bottom of the front of the smock and going around each armhole, ending at the bottom of the back of the smock. Topstitch.

Autumn

I love the fitful gust that shakes
The casement all the day,
And from the glossy elm tree takes
The faded leaves away,
Twirling them by the window pane
With thousand others down the lane.

I love to see the shaking twig
Dance til shut of eve,
The sparrow on the cottage rig,
Whose chirp would make believe
That Spring was just now flirting by
In Summer's lap with flowers to lie.

I love to see the cottage smoke
Curl upwards through the trees;
The pigeons nestled round the cote
On November days like these;
The cock upon the dunghill crowing,
The mill sails on the heath a-going.

John Clare

52
Knitted version of baby's jumpsuit

(9-18 months)
We made this jumpsuit from a thrown-out Shetland wool jumper! (Large man's size). The elbows and cuffs were worn through, but the front and back were in good condition. The knitted bands around chest and ankles gather in the trousers nicely for a snug fit. If the bodypiece is in a plain colour, the ribbed bands can be knitted in matching coloured stripes.

You will need:

Two pieces of knitted material, each 52 x 50cm (20½ x 19½") or the front and back of a large jumper
Matching thread
75gr (3oz) double knitting wool
One set 3mm (2 US) knitting needles

Instructions:

Prepare and cut out the pattern on p.177 (as described on p.63). As knitted materials unravel, it is essential to zig-zag twice around all the edges straightaway!
With right sides together, sew centre front seam (x-a) and centre back seam (y-b). Sew inside leg seam. Start at the bottom of one leg, sew across the crutch and down to the bottom of the other leg. See Diagram 1 on p.64 (Baby's jumpsuit).
To knit the band around the chest, cast on 116 sts over three knitting needles. Knit 22 rounds in K2 P2. Cast off.
To knit the ankle bands, cast on 44 sts over the three knitting needles and knit 12 rounds in K2 P2. Cast off. Make one more ankle band.
Run a gathering thread round the top edge of the body piece and draw it together to fit the slightly stretched chest band. Sew the band onto the body piece. With a gathering thread, gather each bottom legseam onto an ankle band. Stretch each ankle band slightly as you sew them onto the trouser leg.
Knit four straps: for each strap, cast on 6 sts and knit in K2 P2 until the strap is 30cm (12") long. Cast off.
Sew the straps onto the chest band 4cm (1½") on either side of the centre back and centre front.

53
Pull-up: scarf and hat all in one!

This is an incredibly easy way to make a scarf and hat in one go! As girls grow older they often do not like to wear hats any longer and this is a very good alternative. On milder days you wear the pull-up just like a big collar and on colder days you pull it up over your head like a hood. As the knitting pattern is very straight forward and simple, an older child could make a pull-up for an adult. It can be knitted on two knitting needles or in a round. Made in mohair wool, the pull-up looks especially nice! However, sensitive skins might not like tickly wool. You would have to use wool which is soft and smooth.

You will need:

110gr (4oz) chunky knit wool or mohair
1 pair or 1 set 6½mm (10 US) knitting needles

Instructions:

Cast on 80 sts. If you are working in a round, divide the sts over 3 knitting needles. Work in K2 P2 rib until the knitting measures 40cm (16"). Cast off loosely. If you were knitting on two needles, sew the knitted piece up to form a tube. Sew in threads

and try out your pull-up on a cold day!

54
Slippers – socks – baby bootees

With the same basic pattern, there are several possibilities! Make either some tiny baby bootees, socks or slippers for a 1 to 2½ year old. Slippers for yourself or bedsocks for grandmother. The pattern is so simple that an older child could make any of these quite easily. If you like stripey socks, this is a good way of using up your bits and pieces of wool.

You will need:

For babies' bootees approx size 1 – 4 months
20gr (1oz) 4 ply baby wool
1 pair of 3mm (2 US) knitting needles

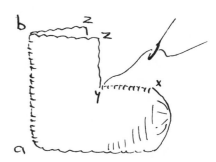

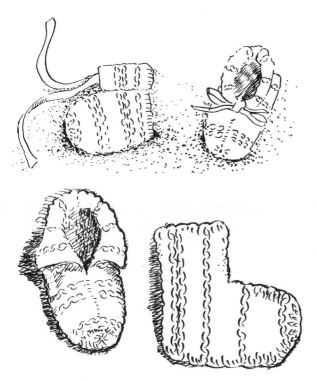

Instructions:

Cast on 56 sts and knit 26 rows in plain knitting. At the beginning of the next two rows cast off 12 sts and carry on knitting with the left over 32 sts. Knit 22 rows and decrease as follows:

1st row: K 2 sts tog and repeat until the end of the row (16 sts left).

2nd row: Purl

3rd row: K 2 sts tog and repeat until the end of the row (8 sts left).

4th row: Purl

Break the wool, leaving about 15cm (6"). Run the wool through the 8 sts, pull together and sew in securely on the wrong side of the sock. Sew up the middle front section (x-y) and the back seam (a-b) as shown on Diagram 1.

If you would like your work to be a sock, sew up the front seam from y to z (see Diagram 2).

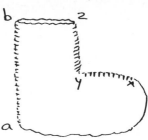

If you would like it to be a bootee with a tie ribbon, fold the top edge (z to b) down, sew it onto the sock and thread a piece of ribbon through it.

Socks or slippers for a 1 – 2½ year old

You will need:

50gr (2oz) double knitting wool
1 pair of 4mm (5 US) knitting needles
1 piece of leather about 15 x 15cm (6 x 6")
(Chamois window cleaning leather works very well if you can't get hold of other leather!)
Strong thread

Instructions:

Follow the instructions given for the baby bootee. As you are using bigger knitting needles and thicker wool, your sock will be much bigger with the same number of stitches given for the bootee. Sew the sock up as shown in Diagram 1 if you want to make slippers.

If you want to make socks, sew up as shown in Diagram 2.

To make soles for the slippers, put one sock on your child's foot and stand the child on a piece of paper. Draw around the foot with a pencil. This is your pattern for the soles.

Cut out the paper pattern twice and draw the outline of the sole onto the leather, taking great care to put the paper pattern the right way up first and then turning it over, so as not to end up with two right or two left feet!

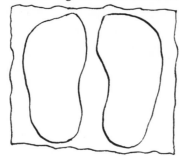

With some strong thread, sew the soles onto the bottom of the socks using an over stitch.

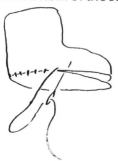

If you like, you can make a pom-pom (see p.138) from the same wool that you used to knit the slipper, and sew it onto the front of the slipper as a decoration.

Adults bedsocks

Especially appreciated by grandparents!

You will need:

100gr (3½oz) double knitting wool
1 pair of 4mm (5 US) knitting needles

Instructions:

Cast on 80 sts and knit 40 rows. At the beginning of the next 2 rows cast off 16 sts. Carry on knitting until you have the required length of your sock. (To check, fold the sock in half as if you were sewing it up – see Diagram 1.) Decrease and finish off your sock as described for the baby bootees.

55
Crocheted slipper variations

With the same basic pattern, you can make these slippers in any size you wish! As you can see from the illustrations, the slippers can be finished off in quite a few different ways. Choose the one that suits you best. The slippers have a sheepskin sole and can be crocheted either plain or in several colours. If you cannot get hold of any sheepskin, you can crochet soles.

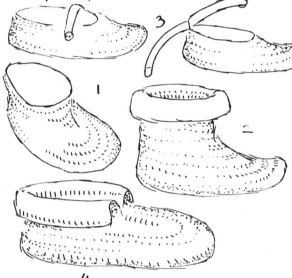

Instructions:

Stand the child on a piece of paper and draw around his or her foot with a pencil. Even out any shaky lines and you will have the pattern for the sole of the slippers. Make sure the soles are not too narrow! Cut out two soles from the sheepskin. (When drawing around the paper pattern, make sure that you turn the paper over after having drawn the first foot, or you will end up with two right or two left soles!)

You will need:

For a slipper size 28 contintental (8):
One piece of sheepskin 20 x 18cm (8 x 7")
50gr (2oz) double knitting wool
3.50mm (E US) crochet hook
Leather puncher

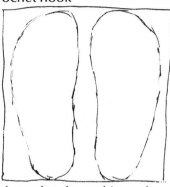

Cut the soles out from the sheepskin and with a leather puncher, punch 3mm (1/8") holes all around the edge of the sole, about 5mm (3/16") apart from each other.

To crochet the slippers use treble crochet stitch.
Starting at the centre of the back (heel), crochet around the edge of the leather sole, one stitch in each hole. Work a second round on top of the first round. Work the third round and when you come to the front end of the slipper, start to shape the toe by working only 3 sts into 5 sts (missing out every other stitch).

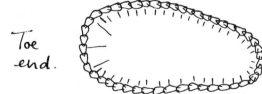

Toe end.

In the next three rounds decrease 5 sts at the toe end of the slipper, in the way described above, e.g. missing out every other st five times.

Your slipper looks like this.

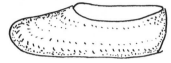

For quick slip-on slippers you do not need to do any more. For slipper no. 3 (see illustration) crochet a strap and sew it in the appropriate place.

If you are making small slippers for a baby or toddler, the size of the opening left is just right for continuing to add more rounds for the opening round the ankle.

If you are making a larger size slipper you have to decide how wide you want the opening around the ankle to be. (It is important not to make it too small so that the child can put his or her slippers on easily.) Sew up the gap created in the centre front with a few sts.

Carry on adding more rounds around the leg opening until the slipper is as high as you like it. To make slipper no. 4 crochet backwards and forwards when making the piece around the ankle and leave the centre front open. For very small slippers you can thread a length of elastic or tie a ribbon through the ankle opening, to stop the slipper from being kicked off!

To crochet a sole (if you cannot find any sheepskin).

Use a double thickness of wool.

First make a length of chain stitch. This must be as long as you want the sole to be, minus the sole's width.

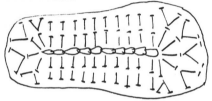

Work along this base chain as if you were working in rows. Into the last chain work enough extra sts to make a fanshape, creating a semicircle. Continue working sts into the chain and make a fanshape at the other end. Join the last stitch to the starting stitch. Work more rounds (increasing only at each end) until the sole is the size required.

56
"Gnome's hat"

Most young children love to wear a real gnome's hat! Parents seem to like it too as it really covers the ears and does not keep falling off. If you wish to knit the hat in more than one colour, you can make it in stripes or even in a simple fair-isle pattern. The size given fits a 1 – 6 year old.

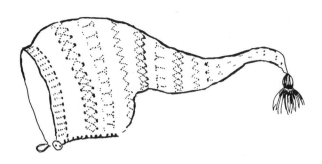

You will need:

80gr (3oz) double knitting wool
1 pair 3mm (2 US) knitting needles for
ribbing
1 pair 3¼mm (3 US) knitting needles
One button
One crochet hook 3.50mm

Instructions:

Cast on 96 sts on 3mm (2 US) knitting
needles.
Knit 20 rows in K1 P1.
Change to 3¼mm (3 US) knitting needles.
If you wish to knit the hat in more than one
colour, start to knit the pattern or stripes
from here.
Knit 54 rows in st. st.
Cast off 6 sts at the beginning of next 2 rows.
Knit 2 rows.
Cast off 6 sts at the beginning of next 2 rows.
Knit 2 rows.
Cast off 6 sts at the beginning of next 2 rows.
(You now have 60 sts left.)
On next right side row:
*K tog 2 sts at the beginning and end of next
row. Knit 7 rows.*
Repeat from * to * 15 more times.
You now have 28 sts left.
Knit 3 rows.

Next row: K2 tog, K4, repeat until the end of
row.
K3 rows.
Next row: K2 tog, K3, repeat until the end of
row.
K3 rows.
Next row: K2 tog, K1, repeat until the end of
row.
K3 rows.
Next row: K2 tog, repeat until the end of
row.
Break the thread and run it through the
remaining 5 sts. Pull together and sew in
securely.
Fold the hat in half and sew the two edges
together as shown in Diagram 2.

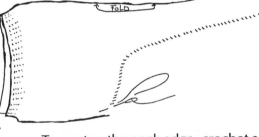

To neaten the neck edge, crochet around it
using a crochet hook. Crochet a loop big
enough to take the button, at the front
corner of the neck edge on one side.
Sew the button on the front corner of the
neck edge on the other side. Make a pom-
pom (see p.138) and fix it onto the end of the
hat (see Diagram 1).

57
Jacket

This jacket can easily be made from a blanket
or even from a cast-off adult's coat! The
seams look best if the blanket stitch is done
in a contrasting colour. If the jacket is made

in a plain colour you can use your imagination and embroider it or sew on some braid. If you wish, the jacket can be lined. A lighter spring and autumn jacket looks nice made from denim or corduroy material lined with thinner cotton. (The blanket stitching in this case should be done with cotton too.) The larger size given fits a 5 – 8 year old child and the smaller one a toddler of about 2 – 3 years.

You will need:

1m (39") wool or cotton material 90cm (36") wide
(If you wish to line the jacket, you will need the same amount of lining material)
Thread in matching colour
Double knitting wool or cotton in a contrasting colour
One crochet hook size 3.50mm

Jacket without lining

Instructions:

Make up the pattern (see p.183) and cut out all the pieces along the **dotted** line. Ignore solid lines. If the material you are using frays easily, oversew all the edges by hand or on the sewing machine. (See "neatening edges" under 'General sewing Instructions' p.7).
For next step see below under "Finishing the jacket".

Jacket with lining

Make up the pattern (see p.184) and cut out all the pieces from jacket material and lining material. Put the lining pieces on top of the corresponding jacket pieces right sides together. Pin and sew all the way around the edge of each piece on the stitching line, leaving one edge open to turn jacket the right way out. Close the edge with very small stitches by hand.

Finishing the jacket:

With the double knitting wool or cotton sew around all the pieces using blanket stitch, about 1cm (³⁄₈") deep.

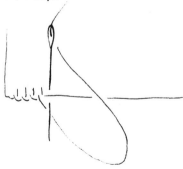

When all the edges of every piece are decorated with blanket stitch, crochet the pieces together (matching letters) using a chainstitch.

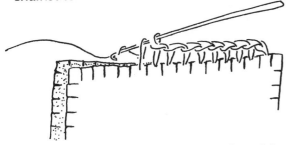

Now crochet around the bottom edge of the jacket and up on front piece around the hood and down the other front piece. Finally around each sleeve.

Crochet two cords each about 35cm (14") long for the larger jacket and 25cm (10") long for the toddler's jacket. Fix one cord to each front piece at the top to tie. If you like make a tassel for the end of each tie.

Fix a short cord (about 10cm (4") long) to the top of the hood and put a tassel on the end of this cord too.

58
Baby's and toddler's sleeping bag

Make this sleeping bag and your baby or toddler will always feel cosy in bed and will never lie there cold and uncovered. It also stops lively toddlers from climbing out of their cots.

The toddler's size sleeping bag has an open-ended zip which runs from top to bottom and therefore cannot easily be undone by the child. For the smaller baby the bag can be made from thick woollen material which makes it ideal for going out in the pram on a cold day. As the child will spend many hours in the sleeping bag, it is very important not to use any synthetic material so that the skin can breathe. Suitable materials are: fine wool, brushed cotton, flannelette, viyella or quilted cotton. The small size is for a baby about 4-9 months. The large size is for a toddler about 1-3 years.

You will need: (for small size)

80cm (31½") material 90cm (36") wide
80cm (31½") lining material 90cm (36") wide
Matching thread
One zip 50cm (19¾") long
2.2m (6ft 4") bias binding, 12.5mm (½") wide, in a contrasting colour

You will need: (for larger size)

2.2m (2yds 12") material 90cm (36") wide
2.2m (2yds 12") lining material 90cm (36") wide
Matching thread
One open-ended zip 60cm (23½") long
2.4m (7ft) bias binding 12.5mm (½") wide, in a contrasting colour

Instructions:

Make up the pattern (see p.185) and cut out all the pieces from the material and the lining (quilted materials won't need lining). With right sides together, pin and sew up both side seams from the underarm edge to the bottom edge of the sleeping bag. Pin and sew shoulder seams. Pin and sew centre front seam from the bottom edge to letter x. Sew along the bottom edge. Press seams open.

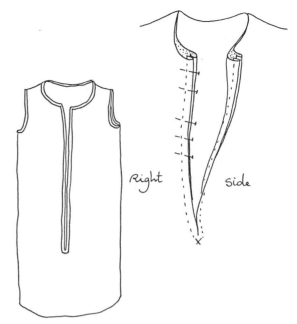

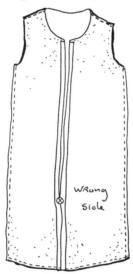

Pin, tack and sew the zip into the centre front opening.

Important! For large sleeping bag only:

Sew the open-ended zip into the sleeping bag so that it closes at the foot end, i.e. you pull the zip downwards to close it.

Repeat exactly the same with the lining pieces. Turn both sleeping bags right side out. With wrong sides together, pin the lining into the sleeping bag, matching all edges and seams. Tack around the neck edge and armholes.
Turn in the edges along the zip opening and tack them together.

Bind the armholes with bias binding. Bind the neck edge and both edges along the zip opening in the centre front with bias binding.

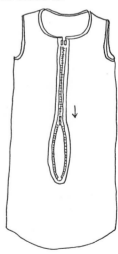

59
Baby's woollen pants

The pattern for these woollen pants has proved to be most useful and effective as an alternative to rubber pants which can cause nappy rash and skin irritations very easily. As pure wool has the unique quality of absorbing moisture (up to 40% of its weight) and of keeping warm even when it is damp, it is very efficient when worn over nappies. They don't become smelly for a long time because the fibre of the wool is able to absorb smells and neutralise them. The woollen pants let the skin breathe, prevent the nappies from becoming cold and absorb moisture so that their dampness does not penetrate through to the outer layers of clothing.

The size given is for about 4-18 months old.

You will need:

80gr (3oz) double knitting wool (pure wool)
1 pair no. 4mm (5 US) knitting needles
1 set no. 3mm (2 US) knitting needles for the borders around waist and legs

Instructions:

Cast on 50 sts and knit 84 rows. This should more or less be a square.

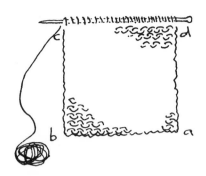

Test it as seen in diagram.

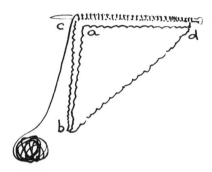

And knit a few rows more or less to make a square. (Corner (A) should meet corner (C) when folded over so that sides A to B and B to C are the same length.)

Cast off 25 sts and carry on knitting with the remaining 25 sts. Knit 42 rows (or halve the number of rows of the first square if you have had to adapt it. Cast on 25 sts to form a Z shape.

Knit 84 rows (or the same number as in the first square).

Cast off.

Now comes the tricky bit. See diagram 3 how to fold and sew the pants together.

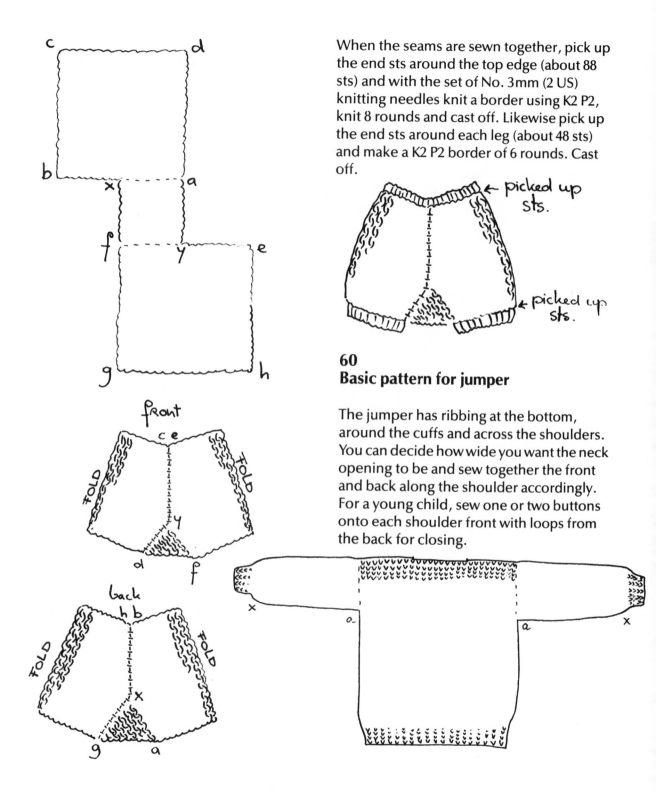

When the seams are sewn together, pick up the end sts around the top edge (about 88 sts) and with the set of No. 3mm (2 US) knitting needles knit a border using K2 P2, knit 8 rounds and cast off. Likewise pick up the end sts around each leg (about 48 sts) and make a K2 P2 border of 6 rounds. Cast off.

60
Basic pattern for jumper

The jumper has ribbing at the bottom, around the cuffs and across the shoulders. You can decide how wide you want the neck opening to be and sew together the front and back along the shoulder accordingly. For a young child, sew one or two buttons onto each shoulder front with loops from the back for closing.

90

Instructions:

Front and back

Cast on the number of sts needed to get the right width (see p.92 how to work out stitch numbers).

K 5 cm (2") in K1 P1 (for a baby's jumper K 3 cm (1⅜") in K1 P1).

Carry on knitting in st. st. until 7 cm (2¾") below the shoulder line. (For a baby's jumper, knit to 4 cm (1½") below the shoulder line.)

Knit these last 7 cm (2¾") (or 4 cm (1½") for a baby) in K1 P1. Cast off loosely.

Sleeves

Cast on the number of sts needed for the width of the sleeve around the armhole. Knit the length of the sleeve minus the ribbing around the cuff in st. st. (a-x) ending on a wrong side row.

Next row *K2, K2tog.* Repeat from * to * until the end of the row. Carry on knitting in K1 P1 for another 4 cm (1½"). (For a baby's jumper make the K1 P1 cuff only 2½ cm (1") long.)

To make up

Sew together the shoulder seams on each side as far as you wish towards the neck opening. Sew in the sleeves. Join the sleeve and side seams. If you use buttons sew them onto the jumper front and make corresponding loops on the back.

61
How to knit a jumper in the right size

Once you know how to work out your own pattern, knitting becomes great fun! Given here is the basic pattern for a jumper which can be made with or without sleeves. This jumper looks nice on a baby or an adult! You can make it with thick or thin wool or cotton. To be sure the jumper will fit the child for whom it is intended, you need to measure a jumper that fits the child really well. To do this, draw a sketch of the jumper and enter all the basic measurements as seen in diagram.

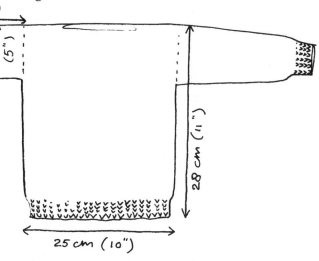

To judge how much wool you will need, weigh the jumper as long as it is knitted with the same kind of wool you are going to use for the new jumper. As stitch tensions differ from person to person, you must find out how many sts you knit to the centimetre (inch). To do this, knit a sample piece: cast on about 30 sts (not so many for thick wool and large needles, and more with fine yarn and needles). The sample piece should be at least 12cm (4¾") wide. Knit until the sample is about 5cm (2") long. Lay the knitting on a flat surface being careful not to stretch it. Insert two pins 10cm (4") away from each other.

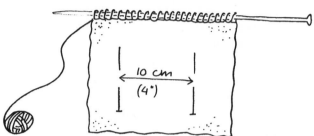

Count the number of stitches between the pins, divide this number by 10 (4) and you will know how many stitches you need per centimetre (inch)! You can now work out how many stitches you need to make the jumper on p. 91 in the right size.

62
Mittens

This is a very simple and straightforward way of knitting mittens. You can either make them just in one colour or in stripes (a good way to use up bits of wool!). The pattern is for a child 6-8 years old. Sizes for 1 year olds and 2-3 year olds are given in brackets.

You will need:

50gr (2oz) double knitting wool
1 pair 3mm (2 US) knitting needles for ribbing
1 pair 3½mm (4 US) knitting needles

Instructions:

With 3mm (2 US) knitting needles cast on 48 (34, 40) sts. Work 38 (30, 34) rows in K2 P2. Change to 3½mm (4 US) needles and carry on knitting in garter stitch. Inc. 1 st. at each end of next row. K14 (8, 10) rows.
Next row* To shape the thumb, work with the first 14 (10, 12) sts only, leaving the other 36 (26, 30) on a stitch holder.

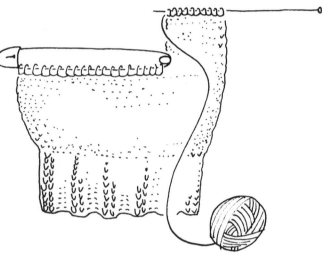

K18 (12, 14) rows. Next row: K2 tog across row. Next row: purl.
Break thread and draw through remaining sts. and sew in securely.
Pick up sts from stitch holder and knit 36 (24, 28) rows.
Next row: K2 tog across row.
Next row: purl.
Next row: K2 tog across row.
Next row: purl.
Break thread and draw through remaining sts and sew in securely.

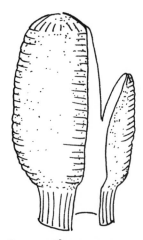

Sew up the seams.

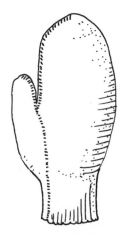

Make one more mitten in exactly the same way except when you knit the thumb* leave the first 36 (26, 30) sts on a stitch holder and knit with the last 14 (10, 12) sts instead of Diagram 1.

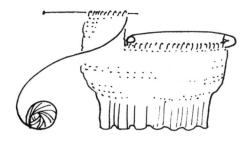

63
Knitted gnome

This little gnome could be a project for a child who has just learned to knit. Some help might be needed with the hat. If you feel inspired you can make a group of them, each one in a rainbow colour.

You will need:

1 pair 3½ mm (4 US) knitting needles
25 gr (1oz) of 4 ply wool in a bright colour and 15 gr (½oz) of 4 ply wool in a cream colour for the face
A little bell for the point of the hat
Stuffing

Instructions:

The gnome's body and arms are knitted in squares made up of 10 sts in garter stitch and 20 rows high. Make six of these. The face, cream coloured, needs 14 sts, 20 rows high and is knitted in st. st. The hat in garter stitch is 16 sts wide. Decrease one stitch by knitting 2 tog. on both sides every 4th row. Continue until you have 4 sts left. Cast off.

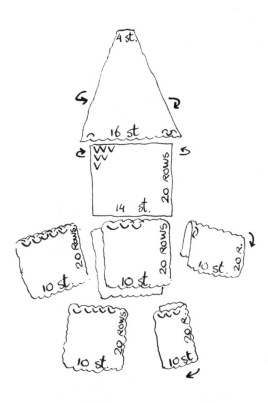

64
Pig

The pig is knitted in rounds. Its legs and ears tend to be a little fiddly to make!

You will need:

Some pink double knitting wool
1 set no. 3mm (2 US) knitting needles
Some fleece for stuffing

Instructions:

To make up the gnome, fold the limbs double and sew along the long side and one short side. Stuff and sew up the other short side. You can make small hands and feet just by tying a bit of wool around the end of the arms and legs.

The body is made of two squares. Stitch around leaving the top open, and stuff. The seam of the face is at the back. Gather the top, stuff it, and gather the bottom. Insert into the body and sew. The arms and legs can now be fastened to the body. The hat has the seam at the back also. Stuff and pull over the head so far that the back touches the body. Sew onto the head. The finishing touch is a little bell sewn firmly onto the very top.

Body:
Cast on 14 sts on 3 knitting needles (5 sts on two needles, 4 sts on one needle). To make the head, knit in rounds K1 P1 until you have 3.5cm (1⅜"). In the next round, double the number of sts by *K1 inc. 1* rep.* to * until the end of the round (28 sts). Carry on in plain knitting until work measures 7cm (2¾") from where you increased. Start decreasing in the next round as follows: Knit 1st 2 sts tog., K5, K2 tog, K5, K2 tog, K5, K2 tog, K5 (24 sts left).
Next round: K2 tog, K4, rep to the end of the round (20 sts left).
Next round: K2 tog, K3, rep to the end of the round (16 sts left).
Next round: K2 tog, K2, rep to the end of the round (12 sts left).

Next round: K2 tog, K1, rep to the end of the round (8 sts left).
Break the thread and gather these 8 sts on a needle and draw together tightly. Sew the thread in on the wrong side of pig's body.
Legs:
Cast on 10 sts over 3 knitting needles and knit 5 rounds in plain knitting. Break wool and thread through sts. Pull tog. and sew in thread. Make 3 more legs!
Ears:
The ears are knitted on 2 needles only. Cast on 8 sts and knit 2 rows in st. st.
In 3rd row: K1, K2 tog, K2, K2 tog, K1.
Next row: purl.
In 5th row: K1, K2 tog, K2 tog, K1 cast off.
Make another ear.
Stuff body.
To make the snout, thread a piece of wool on a darning needle and draw through the very front of the face with a tiny running stitch.
See Diagram 1.

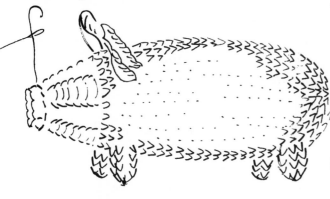

Sew on ears as shown in Diagram 1.
Stuff legs and sew into body as seen in Diagram 1.
Make a short tail by twisting a cord (see p.16) with pink wool and sewing it in the appropriate place!

65
Cat

The cat can be knitted in various 'catty' colours, grey/white, black/white, or all brown. It looks especially nice when knitted with soft, fluffy wool like mohair.

You will need:

About 25gr (1oz) cat colour double knitting wool
1 pair no. 3mm (2 US) knitting needles
Some fleece for stuffing
One thread of pink and one of blue or green wool for the face
Optional: a little bell to put around the cat's neck on a ribbon

Instructions:

For white and grey cat:
Cast on 24 sts in white and knit 12 rows.
Change to grey and knit 34 rows. Change to white and knit 6 rows. Cast off. This piece is the body.
For the head cast on 14 sts in grey. Knit 14 rows. K tog. the first 2 sts at the beg. of the

next 4 rows. increase 1 st at the beg. of the
next 4 rows.
K 14 rows. Cast off.
For the tail, cast on 16 sts. K 1st row. In the
2nd row, K 10 sts and turn (leaving 6 sts
'unknitted'). 3rd row K (this row is shorter
now). Repeat these 3 rows 3 times.

Start sewing the body together following the
diagrams.

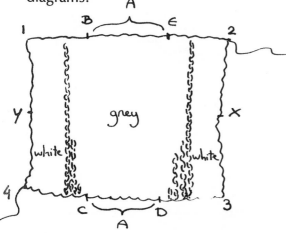

Corners 1,2,3,4 are the feet.
Fold E to X and B to Y. Sew the leg seams.

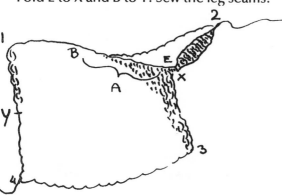

Now sew the leg seams on the other side in a
corresponding way, i.e. C to Y and D to X.
Stuff the body and close by sewing up the
seam at A.

Now fold the headpiece in half and sew up
both side seams.

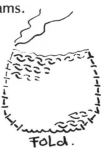

Stuff the head and close the top seam. To
make the ears sew diagonally across the
corners with a small running stitch.
Embroider face.

Sew the head onto the front of the body.

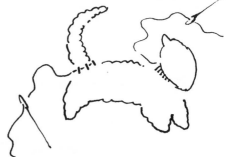

Sew up the tail – it hardly needs stuffing –
and sew onto the appropriate place on the
cat. See Diagram 7.
If you wish put a ribbon with a small bell
around the cat's neck.

66
Finger puppets

Finger puppets are lovely presents for children and good fun to make as they do not take very long. The characters for a whole story or fairy tale could be made. We have even seen an ill child in hospital who had a set of nurses, doctor and a patient!

You will need:

Lots of scraps of double knitting wool in various colours. For the face use beige or light pink wool
1 set of 4 knitting needles 3mm (2 US)
1 crochet hook no. 3 (10 US)
Some cotton wool or fleece for stuffing
2 small bells for the jester
A piece of golden ribbon for the princess's crown

Instructions:

Basic pattern

Begin to knit all the puppets in the same way. Cast on 18 sts over two knitting needles to make sure that the bottom edge is not too tight.

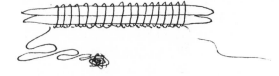

Now distribute the 18 sts over 3 knitting needles (6 sts on each).

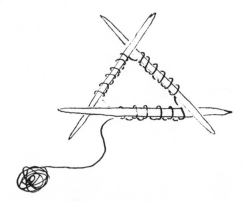

Now you start knitting in rounds using plain st. For the body knit 26 rounds. Change to face colour and knit 10 rounds. For most of the puppets with hats you now knit the hat. For the animals or puppets without hats finish the head off in 3 rounds as follows:
1st round: K tog. the first and second st of each needle.
Repeat this for the next 2 rounds. You now have 9 sts. Break the thread and thread it through the 9 sts with a needle. Pull the sts tog. closing the top of your puppet's head. Stuff the head and thread a piece of wool through the top of the body where it meets with the face and draw together tightly to form the head. Secure thread with a knot and sew ends in securely.

There are many kinds of hairstyles possible. They are all sewn on in the same way: Choose the colour of the hair and thread a length of that wool onto a big darning needle. Make a loop (a big one for long hair, a small one for shorter hair) and right next to it make a small backstitch to stop the loop from sliding.

Now carry on with the next loop etc. until the head is covered. For some dolls you will need very little hair around the hats, for others you might want to cut the loops open.

Here are a few characters – a few ideas:

Jester

Start knitting the body with plain red wool. Knit 16 rounds.
Next round: knit with yellow wool.
Alternate red and yellow rounds until there are 26 rounds (5 yellow ones) ending on a red round. Knit 10 rounds in face colour, change to yellow and start knitting the hat as follows:
1st, 3rd and 5th rounds in yellow.
2nd, 4th and 6th rounds in red.
In the 7th round, K 9 sts in red and leave the other 9 sts on a spare needle. Close the 1st 9 sts to a round and carry on knitting in red.

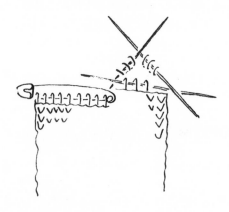

Knit 8 rounds and in the next round decrease:
K2, K2 tog (7 sts left).
Knit 3 rounds and in the next round decrease again in the same way. Knit 3 rounds and in the next round decrease again as above. Break the thread and pull it through the remaining 3 sts and draw tog. tightly. Sew a little bell onto the end of the hat. Now pick up the 9 sts from the spare needle and knit the other side of the hat as described above but use yellow wool.

Stuff and finish the puppet as shown in the basic pattern above.

The Jester has a ring of short brown hair around his hat. Eyes and a mouth can be embroidered onto his face but they are not absolutely necessary.

Boy:

Knit the body starting with 16 rounds in dark green and then 10 rounds in yellow following the basic pattern above. Knit the head in face colour. For the hat change to green and knit 3 rounds. in the 4th and 5th rounds decrease by knitting tog. the 1st and 2nd st of each knitting needle. Cut your wool leaving 15cm (6″) and thread this through remaining sts. Draw up tightly and sew securely on the inside of the puppet. Stuff the puppet and finish as shown in basic pattern. The boy has short brown hair (by leaving the hair loops uncut his hair looks curly!).

With a length of green thread and a needle braces are embroidered over the yellow jumper using stemstitch.

Eyes and mouth can be embroidered if wished.

Princess:

The body is knitted in a soft pink or blue and the head in face colour as described in basic pattern. Follow the basic pattern for stuffing and finishing the puppet. She has long, light yellow hair and around her head she wears a crown made from a piece of gold ribbon which is sewn together at the back of the head.

If wished, eyes and a mouth can be embroidered on the face.

Lion:

Knit the body and the head in yellow as described in the basic pattern. Stuff and divide the head from the body as shown in the basic pattern. Make the ears with the crochet hook:

Pick up first st at the side of the lion's head.

Pull yarn through and crochet 2 chain sts. Now make 3 treble sts into the 1st chain st. Cut yarn and pull through last st. Sew down onto lion's head thus fixing on the ear. Make one more ear on the other side. Embroider the lion's face and mane with thick, dark brown wool.

Elephant:

Knit the body and head with grey wool as shown in the basic pattern. Stuff and divide the head from the body as described in basic pattern. The trunk is knitted in rounds:

Cast on 6 sts over 3 needles (2 on each). Knit 1½cm (⅝") and begin to decrease:
K first 2 sts tog.
K 5 rounds.
K first 2 sts tog.
K 4 rounds.
Cut yarn leaving 10cm (4"). Thread this through remaining 4 sts and pull tog. Sew thread in securely. Now carefully sew the trunk onto the middle of the elephant's face. The ears are knitted in st. st. on two knitting needles:
Cast on 3 sts. In the 2nd and 3rd rows inc. 1 st at each end of the row. With these 7 sts knit 18 rows and then decrease: 1 st at each end of the next 2 rows. Knit 1 row with the remaining 3 sts. Cast off. Make another ear!

Sew the ears onto the sides of the head and embroider the eyes with black yarn.

Witch:

Knit the body in purple and the face in a yellowish-white wool as shown in the basic pattern. Stuff and divide head from body as described in basic pattern. With some very bright green wool knit a headscarf (on 2

100

knitting needles). Cast on 1 st and work in st. st. Increase 1 st at each end of every alternate row until you have 28 sts. Cast off. Sew the headscarf onto the head of the witch and make some hair as described in the basic pattern with orange wool, cutting the loops open.

With the crochet hook pick up a st in the middle of the witch's face using the same method as for the lion's ears shown in diagram 8. Crochet 4 chain sts. Break the yarn, pull the end through the last chain st and sew onto the witch's face as shown.

The witch could have green eyes and a rather large mouth.

67
Arabian belt

This item is good practice in plaiting and gives an exotic result!
A harmonious colour combination is essential.

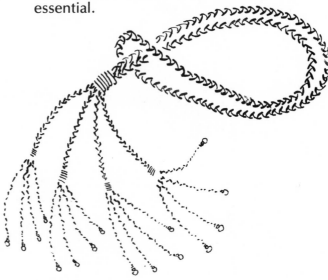

You will need:

24 pieces of brightly coloured wool in tones which blend well or set each other off. Each piece needs to be 3½m (12ft 3") long
Scissors
Large eyed needle
16 small bells optional
Clothes pegs

Instructions:

Line up the lengths of wool.
Leave 55cm (21½") at the ends unplaited and plait the middle part until there is again 55cm (21½") left. Knot some wool around both ends of the plaiting.

Tie the knots together.
It is easiest at this stage to loop your work
through a handle of a cupboard or to
stabilise it in some way.

55 cm

55 cm

Divide the lengths of wool into four sections
of twelve threads. Use clothes pegs to keep
these sections separate. Plait each plait
halfway. Knot some wool around the end of
the plaiting. Divide each of the four sections
again into four and plait each plait to the
end. Tie a knot around the ends.

Wind some wool neatly around the knots
covering all loose ends – this winding can be
about 2cm (¾″) wide. With a needle, thread
in the ends.

Little bells at the ends add a musical note!
The belt is ready to wear.

68
Conker web

In the Autumn spiders' webs show up all around. With a conker you can make beautiful weaving the way the spider does.

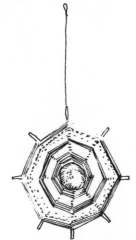

You will need:

One conker
Eight cocktail sticks
Scrap pieces of brightly coloured wool
A Bradawl
Scissors

Instructions:

Make eight small holes in a circle around the side of the conker and insert the cocktail sticks. Cut off the sharp ends.

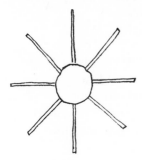

Tie a piece of wool to one of the cocktail sticks. Wrap it once around the next stick.

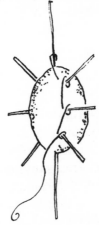

Continue doing this. Push the wool (unlike the spider's web) together, so that you have a continual weaving without openings.
After about ½cm (¼") of weaving, you can tie a different colour to the thread. Make sure the knot is at the back.
Weave with different colours until the conker web has filled up the cocktail sticks about 2cm (1") from the ends.
Make a firm knot around a cocktail stick and leave about 30cm (12") of wool with which to hang up the weaving.

69
Hallowe'en lantern

If you have ever seen a Jack o' Lantern glowing warmly golden in a cold dark night, you will know how friendly he looks with his grinning face.

You will need:

A pumpkin, turnip, or swede
Knife and spoon
Night light

Instructions:

Take your pumpkin and cut a large circle out of the top. Hold your knife at a 60° angle so that when it is put back it does not fall through the hole. This is his hat.

Now gouge out all all the seeds and flesh as far as you are able without breaking through to the outside. When you are satisfied that you have taken enough out you can cut a friendly face on the side of the pumpkin. Place your night light in the bottom and your Jack o' Lantern is ready.

If you have a turnip or swede you may want to carry it about. So make two holes on either side of the top and pull a piece of string through them. Knot the ends. It can now be held up with a stick.

70
Autumn lantern

When the nights are drawing in and the sun loses its strength, it is time to make our own little sun – a lantern. On the Continent, at Martinmas (11th November) the children make their lanterns and take them outside in the dark to walk around in a procession, singing as they go.

You will need:

Greaseproof or tracing paper 30 x 16cm (12 x 6¼")

Thick coloured paper 38 x 24cm (15 x 9½")
Pressed leaves or scrap pieces of coloured tissue paper
One round lid of a cheese spread box, 11cm (4½") in diameter
Glue: Pritt or Uhu
String
Night light

Instructions:

Take the coloured paper and fold over 3cm (1¼") on the 24cm (9½") side. This is the top of the lantern.

Cut out two windows– see drawing. Cover the windows with the greaseproof paper. To decorate the windows you can either glue dried leaves onto the greaseproof paper or tear up little pieces of tissue paper and glue these onto the window.

Overlapping these pieces slightly gives beautiful colour effects. Trim off any excess paper.
Make small cuts – 1cm (½") along the bottom of the coloured paper. Bend the coloured paper so that it fits inside the cardboard lid.

Glue the ends of the lantern together, and fold the bottom inwards. Glue this to the bottom of the cardboard lid. Glue the sides of the lantern to the inside of the edge of the lid.
Make two holes in the top of the lantern, opposite one another and thread a length of string through them. Knot both ends.
Place a night light in the bottom and your lantern is ready.

71
Jack in the box

Here is a very simple Jack!

You will need:

For the box:
Matchbox

Scrap coloured paper
Strong cotton, like buttonhole thread
Glue
Scissors
Needle
For the Jack:
Scrap tissue paper or plain material
A little bit of sheepswool for stuffing

Instructions:

Cover the matchbox with the coloured paper. Glue the edges very well. Stars and moon can be cut and glued onto the front. Line the box on the inside with coloured paper. The little Jack is made as follows: Roll the wool into a little head and cover it with tissue or material. Tie a piece of cotton around the neck. Glue him into the box.

Leave the box out of the cover.
With a needle and the buttonhole thread, make a loop by pricking through the middle of the empty cover, both front and back.

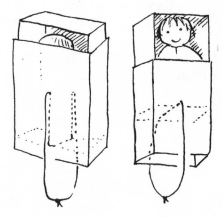

72
Hanging pockets

These are useful for holding all those bits and pieces which lie around with no special home. They can also hold more specific items such as woollen hats, gloves, scarves, shoes or tools of some kind. For the woollen clothes the material can be lighter and the pockets smaller. For shoes and tools you need fairly heavy weight material, large pockets and a length of dowelling to support the pockets when they are fixed to the wall.

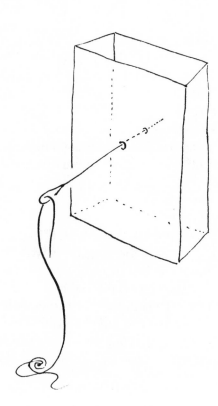

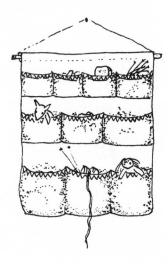

Tie the ends at the bottom.
Insert the box into the cover, pull the thread and Jack comes out of the box!

You will need:

For smaller pockets:
One piece of calico 60 x 40cm (23½ x 15¾")
One piece of gingham 45 x 55cm (17¾ x 21¾")
Some trimming (ricrac, broderie anglaise etc)
Dowelling 40cm (15¾") long x 7mm (¼") in diameter
Light cord ½m (20")
For larger pockets you will need:
One piece cotton drill or denim 90 x 70cm (35½ x 27½")
One piece cotton drill or denim 114 x 66cm (44¾ x 26")
Piece of dowelling 1m (40") x 2cm (¾") in diameter

Instructions:

Smaller pockets:
Take the calico backing and fold over 1cm (⅜") on all four sides. Press. Fold over another 1cm (⅜") on two long sides and one short side. Press and tack. Turn over the top short side 3cm (1¼"). Press and tack.
Take the piece of gingham and cut into three strips 16 x 12 x 21cm (6¼ x 4¾ x 8¼"). Fold over 1cm (⅜") on all four sides of each strip. Press and tack. If using ricrac or other decoration, tack this to one long side of each strip, then machine.
Take the strip measuring 21cm (8¼") and tack to the bottom of the calico on three sides leaving the top open. Measure 3cm (1¼") up from the top of the strip and pin the next strip measuring 16cm (6¼") to the calico. Tack as before. Measure another 3cm (1¼") up and pin the top strip measuring

12cm (4¾") to the calico.
Now machine all the seams.
Having done this, you can decide how big or how small the pockets should be and machine from top to bottom of the strips accordingly. If you want further decoration, you can cut out in felt names, hearts, flowers, etc. and stick them on the space at the top. Take the length of dowelling and cut a slot at each end that the cord can fit into. Pass the dowelling and the cord through the seam at the top and tie the cord ends together.

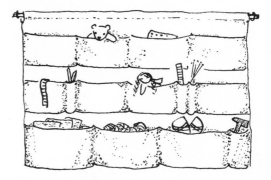

Larger pockets:
Take the denim backing 90 x 70cm (35½ x 27½") and do the same as for the smaller pockets. Take the second piece of denim and cut it into three strips each measuring 20cm (8") wide. These pockets are going to take more bulky objects, so we must make them spacious. Assuming there are to be four pockets on each strip, allow 3cm (1¼") each side of a pocket to make a pleat. This will take up the difference between the 1.14m (3ft 9") length strip and the 90cm (36"). Fold over 1cm (⅜") on all four sides of each strip. Press and tack. Where you want each pocket to be, make a 1½cm (⅝") pleat on

each side and pin. Tack the first strip to the bottom of the backing. Measure 2cm (¾") up and pin the second strip to the backing. Tack on. Measure 2cm (¾") and pin the top strip to the backing. Tack on. Machine all seams.

Take the length of the dowelling and pass it through the seam at the top of the pockets. The projections at each end can be hung on two hooks fixed to the wall.

73
Patchwork

With simple squares children can make all sorts of useful things. Remember to use materials of similar weight and type. Cottons are best. Matching or blending colours look good.

You will need:

Odd scraps of material – material for backing, e.g. old pieces of sheets. Also a thin sheet of foam rubber 30 x 20cm (12 x 8") and dried lavender.
Make a cardboard template 6 x 6cm (2½ x 2½") outside measurement, 5 x 5cm (2 x 2") inside.
When making more complicated patchwork, you make a cardboard template for each piece of material and sew round it, removing it later. As these are simple patterns made with a few squares, we have simplified the process!

Placemats

You need twenty-four squares for this. Place the template on your material. With a pencil draw round the inside and outside squares. The inside square is the seamline. Cut round the outside square. When you have the required number of squares, sew them together in four rows of six squares. Press. Take a piece of backing material 32 x 22cm (12¾ x 8¾"). Lay it on the right side of the patchwork. Machine or sew around three sides. Turn inside out. Cut the thin foam to fit. Turn in the ends of the fourth side and sew together.

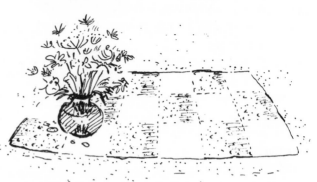

Purse

You need twenty-seven squares for this. Cut your squares as for the place mat. Sew nine rows of three squares together.

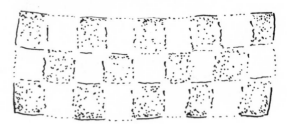

Press.
Taking a piece of backing material 17 x 47cm (6¾ x 18½") place on the right side of the patchwork. Sew or machine round three

sides. Turn inside out. Turn in the ends of the fourth side and sew. Fold over three rows of squares with backing inside onto the next three rows. Sew up each side. Fold the last three rows over to form a flap. Sew on two press studs, one in each corner of the flap, on the inside.

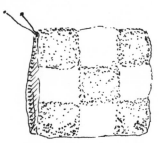

Lavender Bag

You need eighteen squares for this.
Cut your squares as for the placemat.
Sew six rows of three squares together.
Press.
Fold in half with the right side of the patchwork inside. Sew round two sides of the bag. Turn it inside out and fill it with lavender. Turn in the ends of the fourth side and sew.

74
Sandman

Many children like to have something soft and familiar to hold as they go to sleep. This soft little sandman holding the moon in his arms helps to bring nice dreams and will earn a special place next to the pillow.

You will need:

50 x 40cm (20 x 60″) pale blue brushed cotton or flannelette (for softness)
Scraps of felt – soft yellows and a peachy shade for the face and hands
Fleece for filling sandman
Thread
Embroidery thread

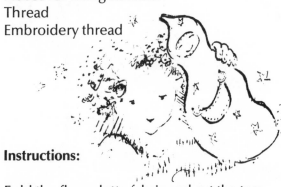

Instructions:

Fold the flannelette fabric and cut the two main pattern pieces (see p.186).
Cut four small stars and two larger ones from yellow felts and also the moon.
From the peach coloured felt cut the face and hands. Pin in position as shown on the pattern. Stitch in place using a small running stitch. Sew the face in stem stitch using pale blue embroidery thread. With right sides together sew the body pieces together leaving an opening at the bottom as shown. Fill lightly with teased and washed fleece. Close the opening, turning in raw edges. Good night!

75
Boot gnome

This little gnome can be made in a very short time and even inspires a four year old to keep his boots tidy! In a large family of course, there will be many gnomes in different colours – even the darkest boot-room will be cheerful.

Stitch from A-B to make the hood, using blanket stitch.
Put the hood over the dollypeg head and draw the thread from C-D together at the neck.
Make a knot and tie with a little bow.

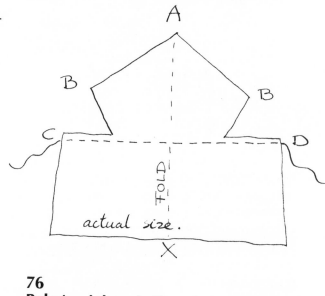

You will need:

One dollypeg (old-fashioned wooden clothes peg)
A piece of felt 7 x 6cm (2¾ x 2½")
Embroidery thread

Instructions:

Cut out the gnome shape in felt.
Sew from C-D with a running stitch as shown on pattern leaving a piece of thread about 2½cm (1") at each end.
Fold along dotted line (A-X) and with wrong side together.

76
Baby's rainbow ball

All the colours of the rainbow come into this little woolly ball. It is an ideal gift for a small baby who is just discovering how to hold things. It is soft to touch and easy to hold (only 7.5cm (3") in diameter). If you like you could put a bell inside to make it even more special.

You will need:

3½ (4 US) knitting needles
Fleece or cotton wool for stuffing
Small amounts of double knitting wool in the following shades:
1. Pale yellow – garter stitch, 8 rows
2. Golden yellow – stocking stitch, 6 rows
3. Orange – garter stitch, 8 rows
4. Light red – stocking stitch, 6 rows
5. Wine red – garter stitch, 8 rows
6. Purple – stocking stitch, 6 rows
7. Light blue – garter stitch, 8 rows
8. Blue – stocking stitch, 6 rows
9. Dark green – garter stitch, 8 rows
10. Light green – stocking stitch, 6 rows
(These colours are only a suggestion, vary them according to what you have available. The important point is that colour 1 and colour 10 should blend to complete a full colour circle when the ball is made up.)

Instructions:

Cast on 10 sts in the 1st colour and work 8 rows in garter stitch. Change to 2nd colour and work 6 rows in st. st. Repeat this sequence of sts with the remaining colours in the order given above.

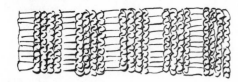

Cast off.
You now have an oblong 'scarf' of rainbow colours. Stitch the pale yellow edge to the light green edge to make a circle. Then gather together one side picking up the st.

st. bands on the first time around and then the garter stitch bands on the second round. Fill the ball with the stuffing (including the bell if you wish). Then gather the other side in the same way and finish securely.

77
Wooden rattles

It is quite easy to make baby rattles and of course, it is much nicer for a baby to get one hand-made from natural materials instead of a cheap plastic one! There are many possibilities for making rattles with beads, bells and rings. Use your imagination to make up other variations. It is very important for the baby's safety to use strong string or cord which will not break and if you are using coloured beads, make sure that they are coloured with non-toxic paint.

Rattle 1.

You will need:

13cm (5") of 12mm (½") dowelling
2mm (³/32") drill bit
Strong nylon thread
Sixteen round wooden beads, medium size
Six small bells

Instructions:

Drill two holes in the dowelling one 8mm (⁵/16") from one end of the dowelling and the other hole 6.5cm (2½") from the same end of the dowelling. Sand any rough edges at the cut ends of dowelling. Thread the bells and beads onto a double thickness of the nylon thread around the dowelling as seen in Diagram 1.

Knot the ends of the threads together separately so that there are two 'rings' of thread running through the beads, in case one of them breaks!

Rattle 2.

You will need:

12cm (4¾") of 6mm (¼") dowelling
Four wooden rings or beads which can slide easily onto the dowelling
Two beads with a diameter of 2cm (¾")
Wood glue

Instructions:

Thread the rings or beads onto the dowelling and glue one of the 2cm (¾") beads onto each end. (You might have to sand the dowelling down slightly at each end to fit onto the beads.)

Dingle-dangle

You will need:

One wooden ring with a 9cm (3½") diameter
Six coloured beads (diameter 2cm (¾"))
Two beads (diameter 3cm (1⅛"))
Six small round beads or bells
One larger round bell
One small wooden ring (optional)
2.1m (6ft 10") thin cotton cord, possibly coloured

Instructions:

With a 2mm (³⁄₃₂") drill bit, drill six holes through the wooden ring spaced out equally. Thread the beads and bell onto 28cm (11") lengths of cotton cord as shown on Diagram 3.

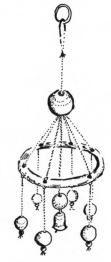

Make knots into the cord, above and below the wooden ring to stop the beads from slipping about. Hang the dingle-dangle up by the small wooden ring.

78
Candle lake

It looks magical to have a bowl of water in which several lit candles float around! Floating candles are very simple to make and look pretty as a centrepiece on a table at a birthday or hallowe'en party. Make star-shaped candles for the Christmas table.

Dip each wick in the wax once to make it stiff. Oil the biscuit cutters and stand them on the aluminium foil. Pour some wax into each cutter, about 5mm (3/16") high. While pouring the wax, press each cutter firmly down onto the foil and hold it for a few seconds to prevent the wax leaking. Wait until a skin has formed on the surface of the candle and then stick a wick into the centre.

You will need:

Small biscuit cutters (as moulds)
Some wax (possibly old candles melted down)
Narrow wick, 4cm (1½") length per candle
A sheet of aluminium foil

Instructions:

Melt the wax in a container that stands in boiling water. If you want to colour the wax, add some wax dye or some broken bits of wax crayon. Cut the wick into as many 4cm (1½") lengths as the number of candles you want to make.

Hold the wick in place and fill the cutter shape with wax to the brim. Hold the wick in place with a match.

Leave to set. When set, remove the candle from the mould and leave it overnight to harden.
Floating candles can also be made by filling half a walnut shell with wax (see p.116 'How to split walnuts in half'). Follow the instructions for the biscuit cutter candles. Do not remove the candles from their shells Just let the little boats float around.

113

79
Magic ball of wool

This is a most original present, especially loved by children who enjoy knitting. The idea is that as the child knits, little presents appear and fall out of the ball of wool.
It is best made from double knitting wool (choose a nice colour!). The little presents should, whenever possible, be chosen to suit the age, taste and interests of the child. The presents can be either wrapped up in nice paper or just used as they are.

You will need:

One ball of double knitting wool
Lots of little bits and pieces such as:
Precious stones, hairclips, necklaces, tiny toys, bells, shells, coins, shiny buttons, sweets (chocolates may melt), flowerseeds, little candles, ribbons, bits of lace, charms, crayons, sellotape roll, notepad, spinning top, yo-yo, beads, tiny animals made from clay or wood, little soaps, etc. Use your imagination!

Instructions:

Start by putting the most special or precious present in the middle of the ball. Wrap the wool around it and keep adding more presents as you wind the wool into a magic ball.

80
Cutting gnomes

These two gnomes hack away at a large crystal. The bells at the tip of their hats are merrily tinkling to the rhythm.

You will need:

Plywood, 3 ply 14 x 20cm (5½ x 8″)
Two strips of wood each 28cm long x 1cm high x ½cm wide (11 x ½ x ¼″)

Fretsaw
Four small pieces of wire
Watercolour
Pencil
Uhu
Greaseproof paper
Handdrill
Two little bells for the hats
Pliers

Instructions:

Trace the crystal. Both gnomes can be traced from the one given. Just turn one upside down. Transfer the figures onto the plywood and cut them out.

Place the two strips as shown. The crystal needs to be in the middle of the overall width. Glue the crystal to the top strip of wood.

Place the two gnomes, straight up, on either side of the crystal 14cm (5½") apart from each other. Mark their placings on the strips. Mark also the crosses where the pieces of wire are going. Mark the place directly underneath these crosses, onto the strips of wood with a small cross.

Drill a very small hole (4mm wide, just over ⅛") through all the crosses.

Lay the gnomes on top of the two strips in the right position, lining up all the holes. Push the pieces of wire through the holes and fix them by folding them tightly back onto themselves.

Colour the gnomes and crystal front and back. You work the gnomes by pushing the sticks in and out. If you want bells on the tips of the hats, drill a very small hole through the tips of the hats and tie the bells firmly onto it.

81
Some walnut ideas

"As soft as silk
As white as milk
As bitter as gall
A thick wall
And a green coat over all."
  Old riddle

Cut the two strips of wood. Shape one end of each piece as shown.

Many things can be made from walnut halves. It is not so easy to open them and keep both halves intact, but you can get quite good results by simply pushing a knife into the joint of the shell at the bottom and then gradually forcing the halves apart. Here are some ideas:

1. Gift box

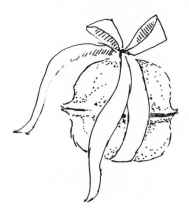

A very special wrapping for a tiny present.

You will need:

One walnut cut in half
A pretty ribbon

Instructions:

Simply put the tiny present into the nut and tie the ribbon round it. (A drop of glue on each side of the nutshell will ensure that the nut will not open by itself!) If wished the nut can be painted gold.

2. Pin cushion

You will need:

Half a walnut
Some sawdust
A scrap of velvet
Thread
Glue

Instructions:

Choose a walnut half that stands well. From the velvet cut a small circle (about 4.5cm (1¾") in diameter). Sew around the edge using a small running stitch. Gather and stuff the circle by pulling the thread around the edge together and filling the middle with sawdust to form a ball.

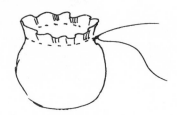

Tie the threads together tightly to keep in the sawdust and glue the cushion into the nutshell, gathers downwards.

3. Table decoration

You will need:

Half a walnut
Some small dried flowers
For a Christmas decoration possibly a holly

leaf
A small amount of plasticine or wax
One small candle
A tiny bit of card
Glue

Instructions:

Put a small amount of plasticine or wax in the
walnut half, stick the candle into the middle
and arrange the dried flowers and holly leaf
around the candle. Cut out a small star from
the card and glue the walnut half onto the
star to stop it from falling over.

4. Tooth fairy purse

This little purse hidden in the walnut is an
ideal place for a child to put his or her tooth
after it has fallen out. Will the tooth fairy
come and exchange the tooth for a shiny
penny or some other treasure?

You will need:

One walnut cut in half
A scrap of cotton material
Matching thread
36cm (14") of very narrow ribbon

Instructions:

Make four small holes in each walnut half
with a drill.

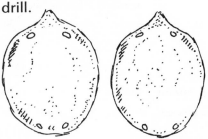

From the material cut out and sew a small
purse to fit into the walnut. Make a hem at
each edge as shown.

actual size.

Cut off about 5cm (2") of ribbon and thread
the ribbon through the holes in the bottom
of the walnut halves to act as a hinge.

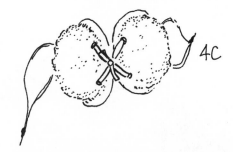

4C

Tie and cut off ribbon on the outside (see
Diagram 4c). Cut the remaining ribbon in
half and thread each length through the hem
of the purse as shown.

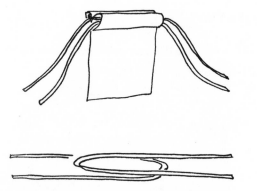

Put the purse into the nut and thread one ribbon through each hole in the top of the nutshell. Tie the ends of the ribbons together to prevent them slipping out again. See Diagram 4e.

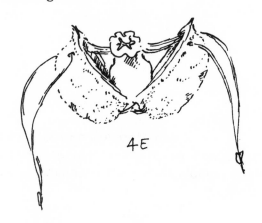

4E

Close the purse.

5. Cradle

You will need:

Half a walnut
Some cotton material
A tiny piece of fleece or cotton wool for stuffing
Thread

Instructions:

Put a layer of fleece or cotton wool into the nut shell as a mattress. Make a tiny pillow and cover and you have a rocking cradle for a doll's house.

If you are lucky you might find another slightly larger walnut half that is just the right size to fit together with your cradle.

82
Advent calendar

"Oh! How many days until Christmas?!"
This question, often repeated, can be
answered by an Advent calendar. Made as a
large transparency (A1 size) it allows one
door to be opened every day. You start at the
bottom, then open the doors around the
outside and finally on Christmas day the
centre panel is opened. Every day one more
of the colour pictures brilliantly reveals

itself. It is very exciting for children. Be sure
to start two or three weeks in advance to
prepare your calendar, as it is time
consuming. Once made, you can re-use it
for several years. If you have a large
horizontal window you can follow our
design, otherwise adapt the overall shape or
make a straight bottom line and stand the
calendar on a table with a little light behind it
(see below)

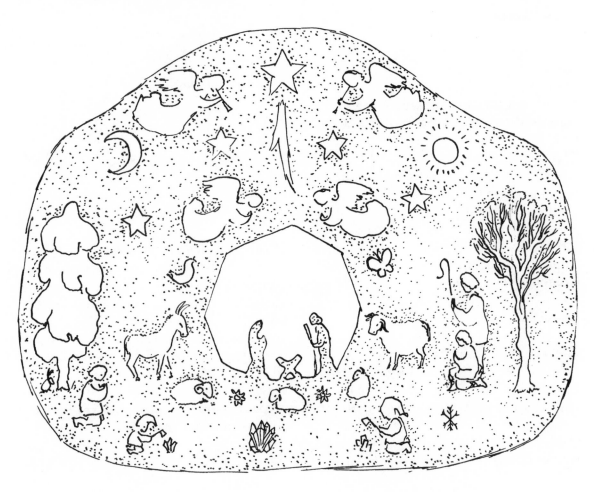

cover the whole with the palest yellow glue round the outside, then work your way outwards with larger and increasingly darker pieces, so as to create a shining, light centre.

You will need:

One sheet of white paper A1
Two large sheets (A1) of thin cardboard, ultramarine blue.
Tissue paper. 1 sheet of as many bright colours as possible; 2 sheets of yellow
Craft knife and nail scissors
Glue – Uhu or Pritt
A1 size piece of clear polythene – if you hang the calendar in the window.
Greaseproof paper
Sheet of glass or perspex about A1 size
Table lamp
Large cutting board – hardboard will do.
Golden sticky paper stars

Instructions:

The pictures look best if they have several colours in them. They enhance each other if you overlap them. Tearing, rather than cutting, can sometimes look very good. The background of the central picture of the stable is built up from larger sections of yellow, golden and reddish yellow. First

Now most of the work is done. Only the doors need to be put on. You can have either removable doors or doors that open. The first look much better but tend to get lost. Turn the transparency the right way round over the light. Trace on the greaseproof paper around the figures. It look very nice if it in not a square but a free, random shape vaguely following the shape underneath it. If you use opening windows (see below) let them open outwards and have the hinge part straight upright. For removable windows you do not need a straight line.

Place this greaseproof paper with the window outlines on the still unused blue sheet and trace the lines firmly. Remove the greaseproof paper.

For windows which open, cut along the outlines but leave the 'hinge' and 'window catch' of the windows uncut.

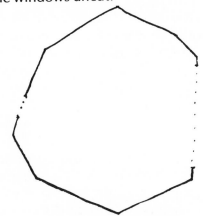

For removable windows, cut the whole window out and with sticky golden stars stick them over the appropriate transparencies.

For the windows which open, put dabs of glue on the right side of the transparency sheet and glue the window sheet onto the picture sheet.

Trim the overall shape into a rounded off form.

Trim any excess tissue paper from the back. If the calendar is placed in the window protect the back with clear plastic. It may be necessary to hold the three layers together with sellotape.

With blu-tack you can place the calendar in position on the window.

If the calendar needs to stand up it may be necessary to glue two firm pieces of cardboard onto the sides. Each side has a large tab to fold back for stabilising the whole calendar. A candle or small light will light up the windows from behind.

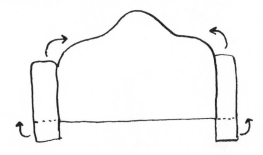

Now you can sit back and enjoy, day by day, your rewarding work.

A painted calendar

If you are not afraid of painting or drawing you can paint or draw a nativity scene, with many details in it.

Put a sheet of greaseproof paper over the painting and draw a large window shape around each detail. Transfer these window shapes onto some card (a nice rich colour) and cut them, but do not cut them right out. Leave a few places uncut so that the windows do not fall out. Cover the painting with the card. Every day a window can be removed and at Christmas the whole front panel comes off. This is ideal for people with dark rooms where every bit of sun-light matters. The calendar can stand or hang anywhere.

Another Advent calendar

This calendar is much simpler than the previous one. Again it is a transparency to be hung in the window, displaying the gorgeous colours when the sun shines through them.

This time both the stars and main figure are cut away. Follow the techniques described in the previous calendar to put the tissue paper in place.

Every star is just a golden yellow. The Mary figure has a red dress and blue mantle. Mary is visible from the first day of Advent and every new day one more star is opened. The doors should be removable, stuck on with sticky gold stars.

83
Advent wreath

Christmas seems to move forward every year. In shops one can buy Christmas trees already at the beginning of Advent. It is very difficult to find the patience to wait until Christmas to put up the Christmas tree but it really only belongs to the twelve Holy Nights. Advent is a lot easier to celebrate if you have an Advent wreath.

On the wreath are four candles. If you have time, it is very nice to set a few minutes aside, just before the children's bedtime, to have the room darkened and the candles lit.

Just one is lit in the first week, two in the second week, three in the third and in the last week before Christmas, there are four candles shining out into the dark to herald the coming of the light in the darkness. A simple advent song is all that is needed to make it into a much appreciated ceremony.

You will need:

Clean, fresh branches of spruce (the Christmas tree type)
Twine
Secateurs
Four red ribbons, each approx 90cm (36") long
Four red candles
Four advent wreath candle holders or firm copper wire – 4 x the height of the wreath
Pair of pliers
It is easy to work on a board on your lap

Instructions:

A beginner's wreath tends to be large, but it only needs to be a circle of about 90cm (36") circumference.

Take a larger branch and bend it into a circle. Tie the ends firmly together with twine.

This is the foundation; it only needs filling out. Always work in the same direction, towards the stem of the twigs.
Place several small cuttings together along the basic circle and tie them into place with the twine.

Turn the wreath and repeat this, filling it out nicely and evenly into a firm, well proportioned wreath. Always cover up the twine with new cuttings. The last ones are a bit more difficult to fit in – just push them into place.
Then turn the wreath over and repeat the process so that it becomes equally rounded all over.
Then tie the red ribbon with bows at four equally spaced places.
In between you place the candles, either in their holders or on copper wire. Hold the copper wire with a pair of pliers. Heat one end of the copper over a fire until the wire is hot. Take the candle and gently but firmly push the hot wire into the bottom of the candle.

Push the wire straight into the wreath. Mind the branches when the candles burn down. If you have no space on a sideboard or shelf, you can suspend the wreath from the ceiling with four longer red ribbons. Tie these onto the wreath in bows instead of the shorter ones.

On Christmas Eve the wreath makes way for the tree, which in its turn lasts through the twelve Holy Nights.

84
Advent tripod

This very unusual and most effective table decoration is quite straightforward and quick to make. Most of the basic materials can be found on a walk in the woods or in your garden. The tripod can be made from any wood (even from bamboo sticks) but it looks especially nice if hazel or birch branches are used.

You will need:

Six sticks 25cm (10") long, each about as thick as your little finger
One smaller, slightly thinner stick, about 10cm (4") long for spike
2.4m (2⅔ yards) red ribbon, 1.5cm (⅝") wide
Strong thread or thin wire
Some small fir branch cuttings
Some ivy (optional)
One apple (preferably red)
One red or white candle to fit into the apple

Instructions:

Tie three of the sticks together into a triangle using the strong thread or wire.

Prepare the spike by sharpening one end of the small stick with a knife.

Now tie together the remaining three sticks in wigwam fashion, putting the spike in the middle – this requires a bit of patience!

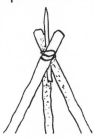

Tie each foot of the tripod to one corner of the triangle as shown.

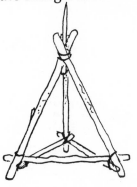

Cut the ribbon into four lengths of 60 cm (2 ft) and tie a ribbon around each 'foot' of the tripod to cover up the wire or thread. Make a bow to finish.

With a knife cut a hole in the top of the apple to suit the diameter of the candle.

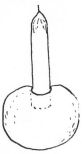

Stick the apple with the candle onto the spike. Tie small bits of greenery around the base of the apple with the remaining ribbon. If wished, some ivy can be wound around the base of the tripod.

85
Crib figures

These crib figures can be made from felt and look very nice under the Christmas tree. You can build a stable for them with some cut-off wooden branches or small logs and pieces of bark. Baby Jesus can lie on a bit of bark in some grass or straw. Put a night-light candle in a small glass jar or in a candleholder in front of the stable to light up the scene. Let some little tissue paper angels (see p.133) fly over the stable. Our children enjoy making a Christmas garden around the crib figures with some moss, greenery, crystals and any little winter-flowering plants they can find. Shepherds can be made in the same way as Joseph but instead of a cloak put a scrap of sheepskin around them.

You will need for Mary:

One 9 x 13 cm (3½ x 5″) piece of red felt for dress
One 13 x 16 cm (5 x 6¼″) piece of blue felt for cloak
One 8 x 10 cm (3 x 4″) piece of pink stockinette
Some fleece for stuffing
Thread
Scraps of light yellow coloured fleece or wool for hair

Instructions:

Twist some fleece into a thick roll, about 11 cm (4⅜″) long and wind some thread around it to keep it in shape. Cut a piece of stockinette into an 8 cm (3″) square and tie this over one end of the wool roll to make a head.

To make the dress, fold the piece of red felt in half and sew up the seam along the 9 cm (3½″) sides. Run a gathering thread around the edge at one end, put the dress over the roll of wool and draw the gathering thread tight around the neck and secure. The figure should stand up.

For the hair put some light yellow wool around the front of the head.

Fold the piece of blue felt around the head and shoulders and secure it in place with a few small stitches. Round off the corners of the cloak at the bottom in the front, as seen on diagram 3. Make two hands by tying a tiny bit of fleece into scraps of stockinette. Sew the hands into the folds of the cloak and with a few more stitches, fix hands and cloak into position.

You will need for Baby Jesus:

A bit of fleece or cotton wool
A scrap of pink stockinette
35 cm (14") of narrow open-weave bandage
One piece of embroidery cotton in a light colour

Instructions:

Make a tiny head by tying a bit of stuffing into some stockinette. Carefully wrap the head with the bandage and create a swaddled bundle. Tie a thread of embroidery cotton crosswise around the bundle for swaddling bands.

You will need for Joseph:

One 20 x 11 cm (8 x 4½") piece of brown felt
One 9 x 21 cm (3½ x 8¼") piece of dark brown felt
One 8 x 10 cm (3 x 4") piece of pink stockinette
Brown thread
Scraps of grey or white wool for beard and hair
One pipe cleaner
One small stick for Joseph to hold

Instructions:

Make the head and body in the same way as described above for Mary. Push the pipe-cleaner through the wool roll for arms. Fold the brown piece of felt in half and cut out the robe (see Diagram 5). Sew up the side seams. Turn it inside out.

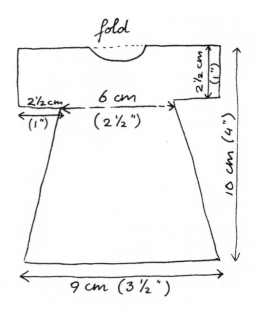

Run a gathering thread around the edge of the neck opening and put the robe on Joseph. Draw the gathering thread together tightly around the neck and secure. Bend back the pipe cleaner if necessary so that the arms are the right length. Put a bit of fleece around the end of each pipe cleaner and tie some stockinette over it to make hands. Sew the sleeves around the hands with tiny stitches. Sew some hair and a beard to Joseph's head. Make a cloak from the dark brown felt as shown.

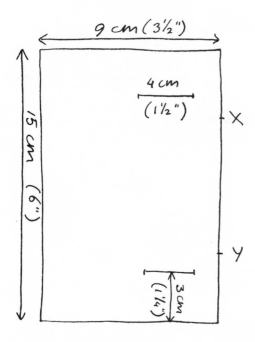

Run a gathering thread from x-y. Put the cloak around Joseph with his arms through the armhole slits. Draw in the gathering thread to fit round the neck at the back. Fold the front of the cloak as shown.

Hold the cloak together with a small stitch and round off the corners at the bottom. From the dark brown felt cut a circle with a diameter of 6cm (2⅜"). Run a gathering thread around this circle 1cm (⅜") from the edge. Draw the thread together slightly and sew the hat on Joseph's head.

Sew the stick to one of Joseph's hands with a few stitches.

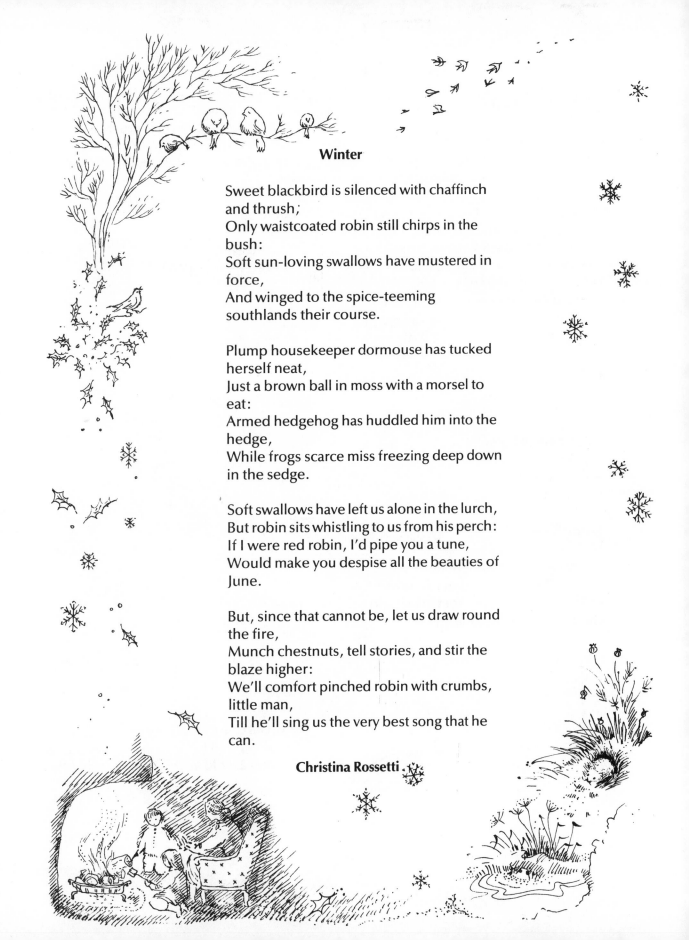

Winter

Sweet blackbird is silenced with chaffinch
and thrush;
Only waistcoated robin still chirps in the
bush:
Soft sun-loving swallows have mustered in
force,
And winged to the spice-teeming
southlands their course.

Plump housekeeper dormouse has tucked
herself neat,
Just a brown ball in moss with a morsel to
eat:
Armed hedgehog has huddled him into the
hedge,
While frogs scarce miss freezing deep down
in the sedge.

Soft swallows have left us alone in the lurch,
But robin sits whistling to us from his perch:
If I were red robin, I'd pipe you a tune,
Would make you despise all the beauties of
June.

But, since that cannot be, let us draw round
the fire,
Munch chestnuts, tell stories, and stir the
blaze higher:
We'll comfort pinched robin with crumbs,
little man,
Till he'll sing us the very best song that he
can.

Christina Rossetti

86
Tissue paper stars

These stars look most effective in the window and really brighten up a grey, misty winter's day! An older child can make them but great care must be taken over folding them as each fold must be very exact. After making one or two basic shaped stars, it is great fun to experiment and make many variations by just folding the paper slightly differently. By altering the length of the sides of the paper or by adding twice as many points to the star, you will get surprising results. Here are some ideas:

1. Basic star

You will need:

One sheet of tissue paper in any size but we will start with a piece 30 x 26 cm (11¾ x 10¼")
Some clear glue
One white sheet of paper

Instructions:

Always work on a white sheet of paper when making the folds as it is much easier!
Fold the tissue paper sheet in half and cut along the fold with a flat knife.

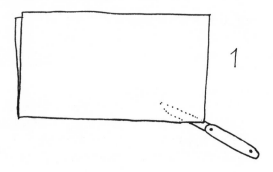

Fold and cut each of these two papers in half again and again so that you end up with eight rectangular pieces which are the same size. Each rectangle will now be folded to make one of the points of the star in the following way:
Fold the paper in half length-wise and unfold again.

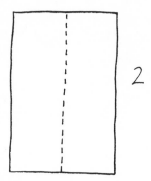

All four corners are then folded in, onto the middle crease.

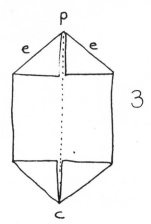

Now call one point C (for centre) and the opposite point P (for periphery) as seen on Diagram 3. Fold edges E onto the middle line.

130

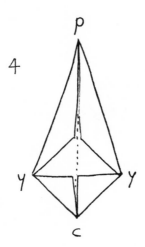

4

When you have glued together seven of the points, the first and seventh point should meet! To glue the eighth point into the star, you have to lift the first section and slide one half of the eighth point underneath.

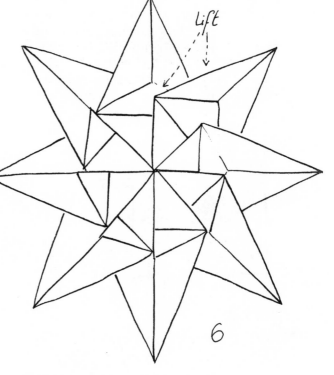

6

When all eight pieces are folded as seen on Diagram 4, set them up in a line in front of you, points C at the bottom and points P on top. This is very important as it is easy to make a mistake when glueing them together. Use glue sparingly. Put a small dot of glue on point C and point Y.

Now to glue the pieces together. The centre points C meet, and the points Y must lie exactly on the middle folding line.

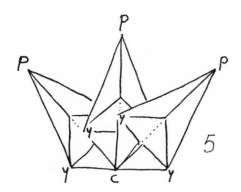

5

(You may have to put a drop of glue here and there if some of the corners flap and will not lie flat.)

Star 2

Repeat the basic star but use a different colour for each point. Glue the points together in this order: red, orange, yellow, light green, dark green, blue, purple, pink.

Star 3

This is very nearly the same as the basic star but there is a folding variation at the end of each point. Take great care not to mix up points C with points P as each of them is folded in a different way. Follow the instructions for the basic star up to and including Diagram 3. Open up each corner fold again and follow Diagrams 7, 8 and 9. Glue the star together like the basic star (see Diagram 5).

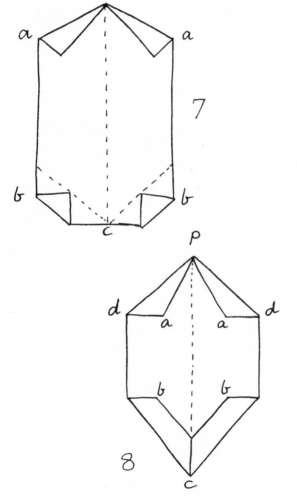

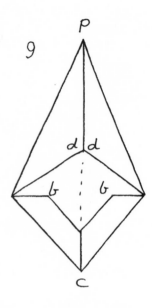

Star 4

You will need twice as much tissue paper as for the basic star.

Now make a star with sixteen points: cut out sixteen identical rectangular pieces instead of only eight. Follow the instructions for the basic star up to and including Diagram 4. Instead of glueing the pieces together now, make one more fold (at c-y) on each point.

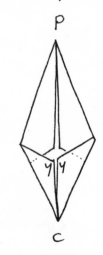

Glue the star together like the basic star (see Diagram 5). As the points are narrower at C, it takes more to get all the way round, back to the first one.

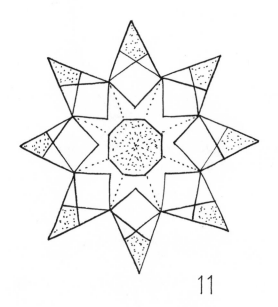

11

87
Tissue paper angels

You can make these lovely little angels with very simple means. They look very delicate if you hang them from a branch of the Christmas tree so that they fly above the stable and crib figures that may stand under the tree. What a lovely surprise it can be for a child to wake up one morning in Advent and find one of these little angels hanging over his or her bed or anywhere else in the house!

You will need:

A piece of tissue paper 30 x 18cm (12 x 7") in a pastel colour
A little fleece or cotton wool for the angel's head
Some gold or silver thread (often sold as 'tinsel-cord' for wrapping up parcels)
A tiny star sequin (optional)
Glue

Instructions:

Cut a circle from the tissue paper with a radius of 8cm (3⅛"). Shape fleece or cotton wool into the size of a marble and put this little ball of wool into the centre of the tissue paper circle. Draw the tissue paper in around the wool and tie the head with a bit of the thread.

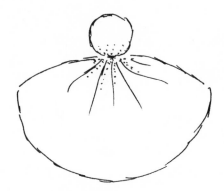

For the angel's arms and hands, make a little twist in the tissue paper at each side.

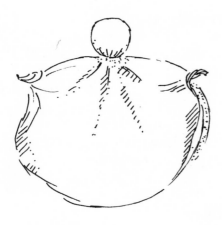

Arrange the dress at the back with two folds so that the wings can later be fixed more easily.

Bunch together the middle fold and tie a bit of thread around it.

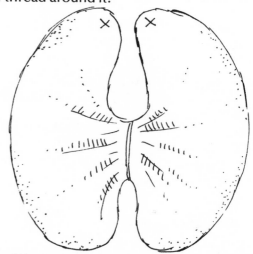

For the angel's wings, cut out a slightly smaller circle from the tissue paper, with a radius of 6cm (2⅜"). Fold this circle in half and shape it by cutting it as shown.

Tie the wings around the angel's neck with a length of gold thread. Leave one end of the thread long so that the angel can hang from it.

Use a little gold thread to tie around the angel's head for a crown (the knot must be at the back of the head!). Stick the tiny star onto the angel's forehead. Put a spot of glue at point x on the wings and glue them together.

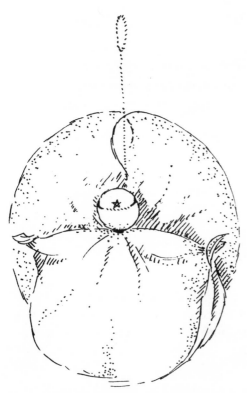

The thread on which the angel hangs must go behind the head and in front of the wings to keep the angel flying nicely.
For a mobile hang two or three angels on a piece of cane.

88
Candleholders

Children love to feel that the darkness is held back by the soft and mysterious light of a few candles. Better still, if they can help with the making of the holders of the little lights!
This can be a good project for the young woodworker.

You will need:

Either a small offcut or a slice of a small log, or even a piece from a branch wide enough to take one or more household candles. Use your imagination when you rummage through the woodpile
Saw
Plane or rasp
Sandpaper
Household candles
Drill bits, the same width as the candles
Linseed oil and a rag to put it on
Watercolour

Instructions:

Cut off the piece you fancy.

Sand down the top and bottom.
Leave the bark on the sides if you like or plane this as well. You can go from the most simple to the most sophisticated shaping here.

135

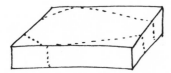

Find the centre in the wood and drill a hole into it just big enough to take the candle. If you have a fancy shape you can paint it transparently with watercolour. Yellows or reds relate to the theme. Lastly you can oil the wood several times sparingly, with linseed oil.

89
Candleholder decoration

This simple candleholder decoration adds a festive touch to your Christmas table. It can be made in various colours to match the candles. Use red beads and green felt for a lovely 'holly' effect! – an easy present that children can make in a few minutes.

You will need:

To fit a medium sized candle:
Seven round wooden beads 1cm ($^3/_8$") diameter in one plain colour
Scraps of felt in a different colour
Some elastic thread

Instructions:

From the felt cut out seven leaves.

The pattern is the actual size.
Using a needle, thread the beads and felt leaves onto a double thickness of elastic thread.

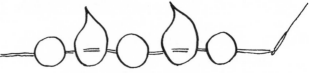

When all the seven leaves and beads are threaded up, tie the elastic thread in a circle, stretching the thread slightly.

90
Twelve days of Christmas calendar

After the climax of Christmas the children sometimes feel a kind of emptiness which can be filled by continuing the present giving with this calendar. In each boot a small present is hidden. In our family we each get a turn opening a present starting with the youngest. The boot-ring looks especially nice if the colours of the boots are like those of the rainbow (light yellow, dark yellow, orange, red, purple, dark blue, light blue, green).

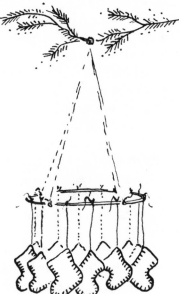

You will need:

Twelve different coloured pieces of felt 12 x 6cm (4¾ x 2½")
Embroidery cotton in matching colours
One wooden macrame ring, diameter 20cm (8")
2.2m (2½yds) red ribbon, about 1cm (⅜") wide
Twelve little gifts to hide in each boot

Instructions:

Cut out the twelve boots using the pattern.

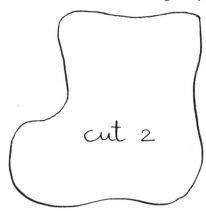

Sew around each boot with a blanket stitch by starting the stitching at the top of the front of the boot and ending at the top at the back of the boot, leaving a long thread which can then be used to hang the boot on the ring.

Hang the boots on the wooden ring, spacing them evenly (see the suggestion above for the succession of colours). You may want to put a drop of glue on the ring for each boot to stop it sliding about. Cut the red ribbon in half and tie it to the ring in four places.

91
Mobile with felt hearts and woolly balls

This is a very easy mobile to make, looks attractive and is especially festive for Christmas using strong red and green colours.

You will need:

A metal or bamboo ring about 23cm (9") diameter which you can get from any craft shop
Card for the woolly balls; a cornflake packet is the right thickness
Green wool for the balls
A small quantity of red wool
Two squares of red felt 23 x 23cm (9 x 9")
Some larch cones are optional
Glue: Uhu and Cowgum

Instructions:

If you have a metal ring, bind it with red wool until the metal does not show through. To hang it up, attach four pieces of red wool about 46cm (18") long, to the ring equal distances apart. Tie together at the ends. To make a green woolly ball cut out two cardboard circles 5cm (2") in diameter. Make a small hole in the middle 1cm (3/8") in diameter.
Taking the two circles, pass lengths of green wool through the hole and wrap it round the card until there is no space left in the centre. Towards the end you will find it necessary to thread the wool onto a needle in order to get it through the small hole. Now, taking some scissors, cut the wool all round the outer edge of the circle. Take a length of wool and tie it as tightly as possible round the centre of the wool and leave the ends long so that the ball can be attached to the ring. Remove the cardboard and fluff out the woolly ball, trimming it where necessary. When you have made four, attach them to the ring equi-distantly in between the lengths of red wool.
To make the heart chains, cut out three sizes of hearts, two pieces for each heart, so that you have small, medium and large.

Take a piece of red wool 23cm (9") long and glue with cowgum the two sides of the smallest heart with the wool in between, the top of the wool emerging 5cm (2") above the heart. Leave a little gap and glue the two sides of the medium-sized heart together. Do the same with the large heart.

Make the other three chains. Tie each chain to the ring at the points where the red wool is attached. Glue the larch cones around the ring on top with Uhu.

92
Embroidered boxes for trinkets

In handwork shops you can buy sheets of perforated plastic for embroidery – they are stiff enough to make into small boxes. You buy the plastic in one large sheet and cut your own shapes. The boxes are surprisingly pretty and do not take long to make.

You will need:

Embroidery plastic 30 x 5cm (12 x 2")
Oddments of double knitting wool for embroidery in matching colours
Embroidery needle

Instructions:

Cut six plastic squares of 5 x 5cm (2 x 2"). With a double thread of double knitting wool start embroidering with the darkest colour.

Cover just a plastic bar, then a hole, again a bar, then a hole. Continue until one row has been done. A zig-zag pattern appears.

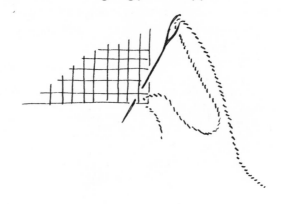

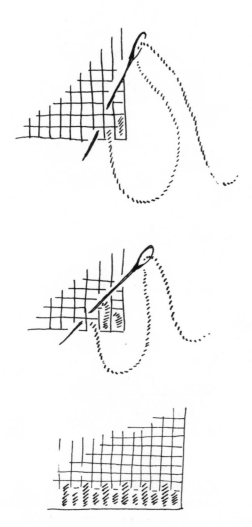

The third row is for your third colour. Continue to cover the whole panel in this way. Cover the plastic at the very top by a line of single stitches. Finish the back neatly so that you do not have to line the box. Repeat this pattern four times. For the top and bottom you can start to improvise.

This is just an example.
Cover all the edges of the top lid as this will show up most of all.
To assemble your box you overstitch the four sides into a box shape. Fit and sew the bottom in place. The lid needs sewing only on one side.

You can use backstitch if you find the zig-zag pattern too difficult.

Then use your next darkest colour but cover only one hole every time, so that the zig-zag pattern is carried on.

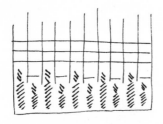

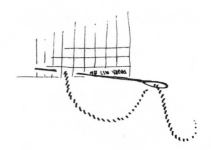

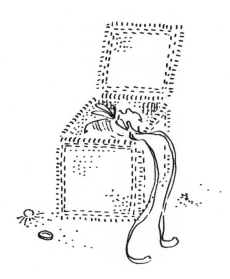

24 x 17 cm (9½ x 6¾") cotton material
One teaspoon full of dry sand (to weigh the gnome down)
7 x 7 cm (3 x3") pink stockinette material for the head
A little fleece for the gnome's beard and for stuffing the head
Thread

93
Climbing gnome

Children love to make the gnome climb rapidly to the top by pulling first one string and then the other. It's even more fun to watch the gnome rush down again the moment the strings are slackened. This toy can also be made with other climbers (even animals) so long as the essential feature is there, which is a hole drilled at an angle at the end of its arms.

You will need:

Two pieces of dowelling, diameter 12 mm (½"), each 10 cm (4") long
One 3 mm (⅛") drill bit
2.2 m (7 ft 3") thin string. (String must be very smooth!)
Five small round wooden beads to thread on the string

Instructions:

Make up pattern for gnome and cut out all the pieces from the cotton material (see back). With right sides together sew around the edge of the gnome's body (a-b) leaving the top edge and armholes open.

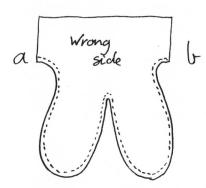

Fold the hat in half and sew up the back seam with right sides together.

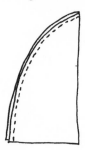

Clip the curves, especially round the legs of the bodypiece, and turn both hat and body the right way out. Drill three holes into one of the dowelling pieces, for hanging up the gnome.

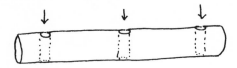

Drill two holes into the other piece of dowelling. It is **very** important that they are at an angle. This is for the arms.

Make the gnome's head, with a small ball (about 3cm (1¼") diameter) of fleece or cotton wool. Tie the stockinette material around this ball.

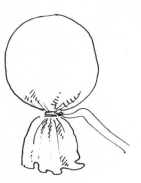

Sew some more fleece around the head for hair and a beard. Fold in the bottom edge of the hat and secure the hat on the gnome's head with a few stitches.

Put ½ teaspoon of sand into each leg of the body. Carefully centre the head and arrange the folds of the cloth (below the neck) around the back and the front of the armstick. Sew the bodypiece around the armstick, folding in all edges and securing the head firmly in the middle.

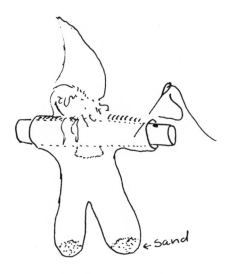

← sand

94
Doll

This is one of the most important toys for boys and girls alike, as it is an image of the human being and can be used as an alter ego. The doll should not be too life-like but should leave the child free to use his or her imagination. This doll is a lovely round, soft, cuddly person who will be a real friend for a long time.

To hang the climbing gnome up, thread the strings through the holes of the dowelling pieces and secure with beads as shown.

You will need:

White stretchy cotton for the underneath head layer (an old vest is ideal)
Flesh coloured stockinette 50 x 50cm (19½ x 19½") is enough for a 12" doll
Fleece for stuffing, washed and carded
Strong white button thread
Wool for the hair, 2 ply or 3 ply or mohair

So that you can make the doll any size you want, no measurements are given. Only the proportion of the head to the rest of the body must be calculated. The body is 1½ times the length of the head, and the legs are the same length as the body. If you are making a baby doll, the arms should not meet on top of the head. If it is a child doll then the arms should be a little longer. So, if you make a doll whose head-height is 5cm (2"), the body will be 7½cm (3") long and so will the legs. The arms will also be about 7½cm (3") long.

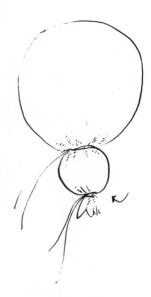

With a length of button thread tie tightly round the neck of the head ball making sure that some wool is hanging down in the part below the neck.

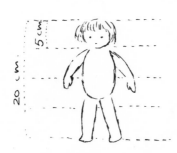

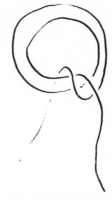

Instructions:

The head:
With the white stretchy cotton underlayer, sew a pouch. This should be the same width as the doll's body and about the same length. Taking some fleece stuff it into the pouch, adding more and more until it is really firm. If the head is too soft, it will lose its shape very quickly.

The firmness of this part ensures that the head does not wobble. Stuff more wool into this part if you think it is not firm enough. Take more button thread and tie up the end of the material. Now with ordinary thread make a neat edge having tucked the ends of the material into the neck.

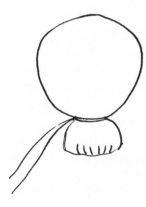

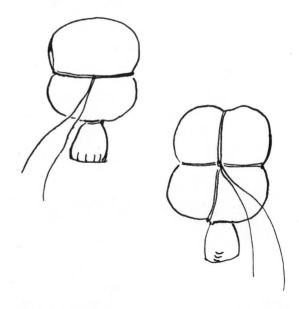

Fasten a length of button thread to where an ear would be on your head ball (half way down the ball). Pull it horizontally round the head once or twice as tightly as you can and fix it where the other ear would be. This gives you the eye line.

Attach another length of thread at the ear position. Pass it over the top of the head pulling it tightly, and attach to the other ear position. Now pass it under the chin through the neck and up again to the first ear. Pull tightly and attach it.

To shape the back of the head, pull the thread down to make a nicely shaped skull.

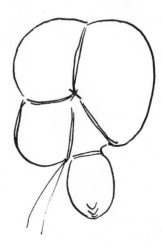

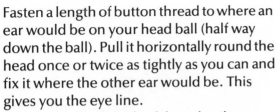

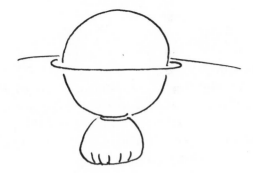

Now cut the stockinette layer for the head. The fabric should be stretched horizontally around the head. Allow 2½cm (1") above the head and 4cm (1½") below for the neck.

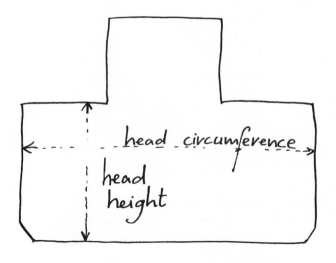

head circumference

head height

Now stick pins in where you think the eyes and mouth should be. With one stitch for each eye, pull the thread (blue or brown) through from the back of the head behind the ear, having knotted the end firmly first. Your needle should appear where the pin is. Now push the needle back again to behind the ear. Pull very tightly and you will have an eye socket. Attach the thread. Repeat for the other eye.

With red thread, embroider a small mouth. Remember that the eyes and mouth should form an equi-distant triangle.

Pull the fabric across the face tightly. Overlap it at the back of the head. Turn the raw edge under and pin. Pull the top flap to the back of the head tightly, turn in the raw edges and pin. Now sew all the seams. With a running stitch sew round the neck and pull tight. Attach the thread.

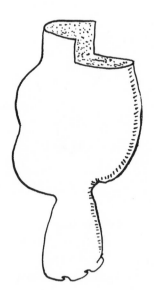

The body:
Remembering that the body is 1½ times the length of the head, and also the legs are 1½ times the length of the head, cut two shapes like this in stockinette fabric with the stretch running horizontally.

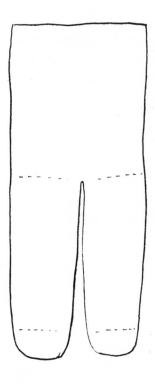

Sew the two sides of the body together leaving the top open. Turn inside out. Stuff first the legs and with more stuffing, stuff the body firmly. Then sew a gather seam across the legs where the ankles should be and draw tight. Also sew across the legs where they join the body. This also enables the doll to sit down.

Now sew the two pairs of arms together, turn inside out, and stuff, leaving the overlapping ends fairly empty. Attach the arms to the back of the 'spine'.

The arms should be about the same length as the body, but allow extra length because they are going to overlap.

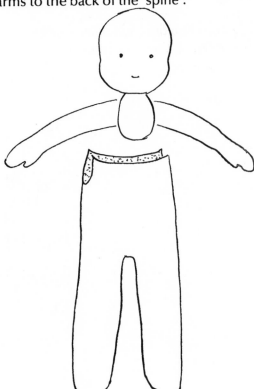

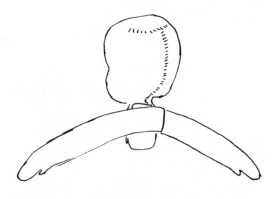

Cut two pairs of arms.

Now take the head and arms and place them in the top of the body.

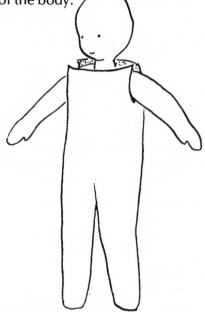

Sew up the shoulders and neck very firmly so that the head sits well on the body and does not wobble.

Sew around the wrists and draw tight to make the hands as you did for the feet. On the feet you can also sew a tuck to make them turn up like this:

The hair can be done like this:

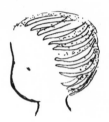

Sewing to a point at the crown from the hair line.

Sewing from a centre parting to a point over the ear.

Alternating loop stitches with tight stitches that fix the loops in place. For a 'crew cut' you can cut the loop stitches.

Do not make the mistake of using wool that is too thick. It will not go through the stockinette. Use 2 or 3 ply. It is helpful to mark the hairline with pins before you start sewing and also to mark a centre parting if you are making one.

Your doll is now ready to be clothed!

95
Doll in a jumpsuit

This doll is suitable for the younger child who is not interested in taking clothes off and on, or who might take them off but not put them on again! It is also a lot easier to make than the basic doll as it needs no clothes and its jumpsuit is its body.

You will need:

A piece of material in a pleasant colour; cotton velour is ideal; 40 x 40cm (16 x 16")
A piece of stretchy cotton 20 x 25cm (8 x 10")
A piece of pink or beige stockinette or similar stretchy cotton material 31 x 15cm (12 x 16")

Some wool for hair about 25gr (less than 1oz)
Thread the same colour as your material
Thread for eyes and mouth
Wool for stuffing
Braid for decoration, optional, 40cm (16")

Instructions:

Make the head as for the first doll on p.144 except that when you cut out the underlayer you are going to make it larger so that it includes the body as well.

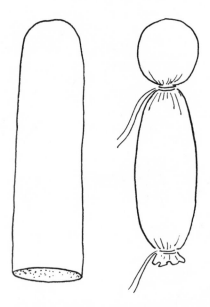

Take the two armpieces and machine 10cm (4") top and bottom on both sides.

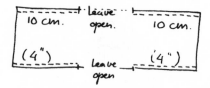

Take the two leg pieces and machine down both sides of the legs so that you have a pair of trousers. Gather the top of the 'trousers' so that it fits round the doll's body.

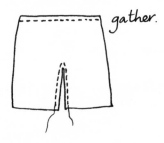

Stuff the body part of the 'tube' well so that the doll will be cuddly. Sew up the end, neatly tucking in the corners so that the bottom is rounded.
Now cut out the jumpsuit.

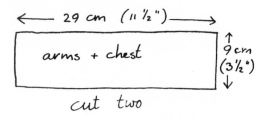

← 29 cm (11 ½") →

arms + chest

↑ 9 cm (3½") ↓

cut two

Take the top and pull it over the doll's body. Then attach it firmly to the neck and sew up the shoulder.

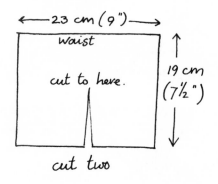

← 23 cm (9") →

waist

cut to here.

19 cm (7½")

cut two

Pull the trousers on up to the 'waist' and attach them to the top.

150

Now stuff the arms and legs loosely with wool so that they are not too stiff and the doll can sit down. Cut out four squares of stockinette 5 x 5cm (2 x 2") for the hands and feet and with a little wool make four balls.

Tuck in the ends of the material on the arms and legs and run a gathering stitch along the fold. Tuck the hands and feet in and sew on firmly.

To make a cap, cut out a triangle from the remaining piece of material long enough along the base to go round your doll's head plus 2cm (¾") seam allowance. Fold and machine from the base to the point.

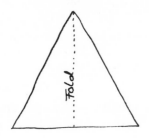

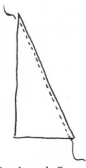

Now attach the hat firmly to the head. Sew some braid round the waist and hat for decoration. You could also sew a bell on the end of the hat.

Cushion doll

This is made in exactly the same way as the jumpsuit doll except that you do not make legs. It is in a little sleeping bag and is very suitable as a first doll. You may want to make the cap shorter so that it is more like a bonnet.

96
Brother, sister, baby

This little family go very well in a doll's house and love to be together. The dolls are easy to make and bigger children could sew them for smaller children.

You will need:

A small piece of stockinette 24 sq. cm
A piece of velour or soft towelling 30 x 26cm
Carded wool for stuffing
Wool for the hair
Scraps of material and braid for decorating

Put the right sides together and sew around the edge leaving an opening at the neck and cuffs. Turn it inside out. Take two little pieces of stockinette and make two little hands stuffed with wool. Sew them into the cuffs. Stuff the body with wool and then sew on the head. From the crown of the head sew with wool down to the hairline all around. Make eyes and mouth with a single stitch of cotton. You can now decorate him. A little bit of braid is very effective.

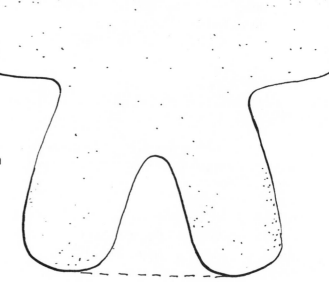

Instructions:

For the brother, cut out a piece of stockinette 7 x 7cm (2¾ x 2¾"). Stuff it firmly with wool so that it makes a little ball and sew around the neck tightly. Cut out of the velour a shape like this. Cut two.

Make the sister in the same way but make her a little shorter. Give her a little skirt.

To make the baby, make the head in the same way. Cut two pieces of velour 6 x 7cm (2¼ x 2¾") and cut a shape as shown.

152

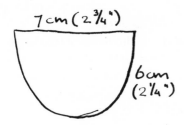

7cm (2¾") · 6cm (2¼")

97
Glove puppet

This is perhaps more of a toy for mother or father to make and use in a puppet show for a small child. It does not need to be at all elaborate. A simple story with very few props and characters will have him or her enthralled.

Put the right sides together and sew around the edge leaving the top open. Make two tiny hands with stockinette and sew them on each end.

Insert the head in the middle and gather the material a little so that the hands are pulled towards the head.

The family is now ready.

You will need:

A piece of stretchy material e.g. from an old cotton vest or pants, about 15cm (6") square
Stockinette, also 15cm (6") square, for the head
A piece 5 x 10cm (2 x 4") for the hands
A small amount of stuffing for the head
A piece of thin cardboard 7 x 6cm (2¾ x 2½")
A piece of thin material 44 x 44cm (17½ x 17½") which hangs well – silk is ideal

Instructions:

Follow the instructions for the doll on p.144, except that when you are stuffing the underlayer of cotton material you insert the piece of cardboard which has been rolled up to fit your index finger. Leave a space in the stuffing so that the cardboard roll can be pushed well up into the head. You may need assistance from somebody to tie the strong cotton button thread around the neck. The tube is now protruding from the neck of the puppet.

Now take the small pieces of stockinette and make hands big enough for you to fit your thumb and middle finger into. Sew the hands onto each end of the material. From below the hands cut the material on either side so that it tapers in slightly. Sew up the seams and hem the bottom.

You can now decorate your puppet according to his or her character. See the drawings for some suggestions.

You must now make sure that the tube will not come out of the head by stitching it firmly to the underlayer. Then continue to make the head as for the doll, having decided what character you want the puppet to be. There should be enough stockinette left over to make hands. Now take the piece of material and fold it in half so that the fold lies along the neck and shoulders of the puppet. Make a hole halfway along this fold, big enough for the neck to fit into. Sew the material onto the neck.

You will need:

A piece of cotton or wool material 23 x 92 cm (¼ yard)
Three buttons, press studs or poppers
Thread to match
Small piece of bias binding for the neck
46 cm (18") round elastic

Instructions:

Cut out from the pattern.

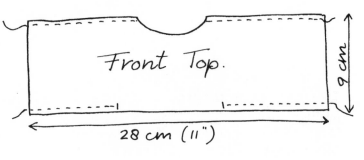

Front Top.

9 cm

28 cm (11")

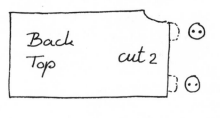

Back Top   cut 2

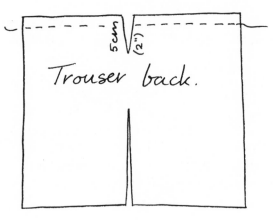

Trouser back.

5 cm (2")

98
Dolls clothes

Children are always pleased to have clothes made for their dolls, especially ones which do not fall apart, as manufactured ones seem to do after a very short time. Some of these designs are so simple, that older children could sew them themselves. Use good, bright colours.

Jumpsuit

This is very similar to the one made for the doll in a jumpsuit, p.149, except that this is made to take off. It will fit a doll 30 cm (12") high.

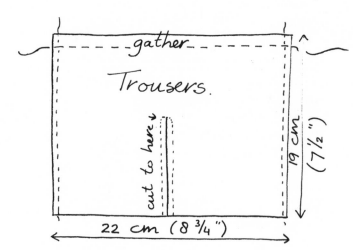

Trousers.

gather

cut to here ↓

19 cm (7½")

22 cm (8¾")

Dress

You can make a dress in exactly the same way without cutting the material in the centre for the trousers.

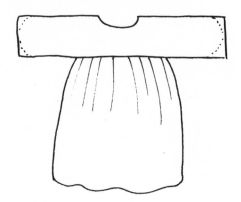

Take the front top and two back pieces and lay them together, right sides of the material facing each other. The two back pieces will overlap in the middle. Machine a 1cm (³/₈") seam on the top and bottom of the arms. Take the trouser pieces and lay the material right sides together. Machine a 1cm (³/₈") seam down the outside and inside legs. On the back of the trousers make a 5cm (2") vertical cut in the middle: Now run a gathering stitch around the waist. Sew the trousers to the top. Turn in the trouser bottoms and arm cuffs 1cm (³/₈") and again 1cm (³/₈"). Hem the seams and thread elastic through and knot it. Take the bias binding and lay it on the right side of the material around the neck. Machine round. Turn the bias binding over and sew it to the inside of the material. Turn the edges of the back opening in twice and sew. Sew on the press studs or buttons. If you use buttons you must make loops out of thin strips of material or use strong thread.

All-in-one pants and vest

You will need:

An old T shirt or vest
50cm (19½") white tape
Two press studs
Thread

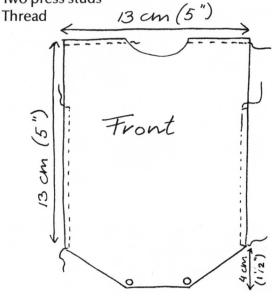

13 cm (5")

13 cm (5")

Front

4 cm (1½")

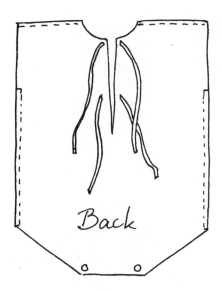

Back

Two press studs.

Instructions:

Cut out from the pattern.
Machine along the shoulder seams and down each side. Turn in 1cm (⅜") and then once more and sew round the neck, back opening, armholes and leg holes.
Sew on the two press studs at the bottom and sew on four pieces of tape at the back.

Here are some simple knitted dolls clothes.

You will need:

Knitting needles 3mm (3 US)
Small amounts of wool

1. Pinafore

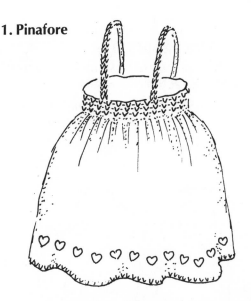

This is knitted in rounds. The yoke-band must fit tightly around the doll's chest. Knit 5 rounds in K1, P1. Double the number of sts (K1, inc.1, K1, inc.1 etc). A simple fair-isle pattern can be used around the bottom. Purl the last three rounds before casting off. Knit braces with 3 or 4 sts to required length.

2. Slippers

Cast on 12 sts. K about 14 rows in garter st. K 2 tog. across the last row – 6 sts. left. Draw sts tog. and sew as seen on the diagram.

3. Hat

Measure around the doll's head. Knit 4 rows in K1 P1 which should fit tightly round the doll's head. Carry on in st. st. to the required length. K2 tog. across the row, and draw together the left-over sts. Sew up the side seam.

4. Waistcoat

This can be made of felt.

You will need:

A piece of felt 15 x 25cm (6 x 10")
Button (optional)
Thread and embroidery thread if you want to decorate it

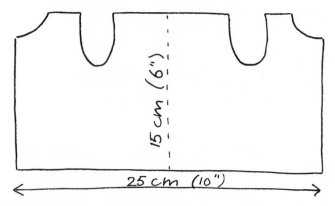

15 cm (6")

25 cm (10")

Instructions:

Cut out from the pattern. Sew up the shoulder seams. Add button and decorate if you wish.

99
Dolls house

This will be greatly enjoyed by little children, especially if you make a doll and a bed to go with it.

You will need:

1 cardboard box approx. 30 x 22cm (12 x 8½") and 26cm (10¼") high
Plain material for the outside of the box
Patterned for the inside
Piece of felt 30 x 22cm (12 x 8½") for the floor
Extra smaller pieces to make the door and windows and pocket for clothes etc.
Glue

Instructions:

Cut out one side and the top flaps of the box. Cut along the two sides of the bottom leaving it attached on the long side.

Now glue your plain material on the outside of the box having cut it 2cm (¾") bigger all round so that you can fold it over and make a neat edge. You can use some braid or binding to glue all round the edges to make it look really neat.

Next take your patterned material and do the same on the inside. Then stick felt to the 'floor'.

Make a pouch about 16cm long which can be sewn onto the longest inside wall. Allow a few extra cms on each end so that you can make tucks along the bottom. The pocket will then be full enough to take the dolls' clothes.

You can fold the house up so that it is easy to carry. Attach a long piece of tape to one edge so that you can tie the house up and its walls will not flap about.
Children will be quite happy with a piece of cloth for the roof.

Dolls bed

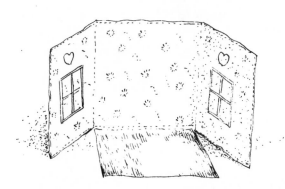

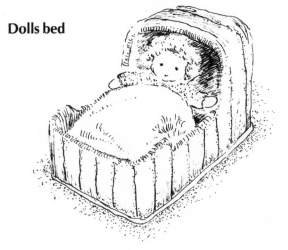

Now you have your basic house, you can make the door and windows as you think fit. You can cut out trees and flowers and stick them on as well.

If you want to make a doll's bed that will fit into this house, get a child's shoe box. You can make a hood for the bed by cutting a strip of cardboard 5cm (2") wide. Place it at one end of the box in an arc and glue both ends to the inside of the box.

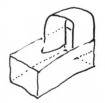

You will also need material to cover it. The easiest way to do this is to use quilted material. This makes it nice and soft with no hard edges and you can glue most of it to the box without the glue showing through at all.

You may need to stitch it where one piece of material joins another.

100
Knitted doll

Using the same basic pattern as the one for the knitted gnome on p.161 you can make a doll. Use wool in one colour for the head and body. Change to a different colour for the feet so that your doll wears shoes and will not lose them! Clothes for the doll can be knitted or sewn.

You will need:

40gr (1¾oz) double knitting wool for head and body
A small amount of double knitting wool for feet, in a different colour
A small amount of yellow or brown wool for hair
One set of 3mm (2 US) knitting needles
Fleece for stuffing

Instructions:

Follow the instructions for the knitted gnome on p.161. Change colour where the pattern says 'To shape the foot'. Do not knit the hat. Stuff the doll like the gnome and turn to p.148 where you will find instructions on how to make the doll's hair.
Your doll is now ready to be dressed!

101
Knitted gnome

This gnome has been a great favourite of many children. It can be old with a white beard or young with brown or fair hair. As one child was very fond of crystals, we made his gnome a little rucksack in which we put some precious stones. Another child might like the gnome to carry a little hammer or a hatchet in a belt. The gnome in this pattern is about 25 cm (10") tall. If you wish to make a bigger gnome, follow the same instructions but use thicker wool and larger knitting needles. For a tiny gnome use 4 ply wool and very fine knitting needles.

The gnome can either be made using just one colour for body and hat, or it can be knitted in stripes. Alternatively its 'jumper' can be in one colour and its hat and trousers in a different one – there are many different possibilities!

You will need:

30 gr (1¼ oz) double knitting wool for body and hat
10 gr (½ oz) soft pink or light beige double knitting wool for face and hands
Scraps of white, brown or yellow wool for hair
Four 3 mm (2 US) knitting needles
Some fleece for stuffing

Instructions:

Cast on 40 sts over 3 needles in face colour. Knit 30 rounds.

Change to colour for jumper and knit 20 rounds. If you want to make the trousers in a different colour, change to the trouser colour now. K 12 rounds. Divide the sts in half for the legs. Leave 20 sts on a spare needle and continue with the other 20 sts. K 21 rounds.

To shape the foot: K 1 round. Purl 1 round. Decide which is the front of your gnome.

Arrange the sts as follows: Put 6 sts for the heel on one needle at the back of the gnome. Put 7 sts each on the other two needles.

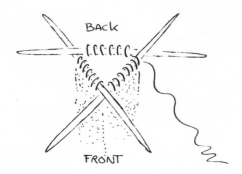

Starting on the first of the two knitting needles with 7 sts, K 6, inc 1, K 1. On next needle K 1, inc 1, K 6. K the 6 sts at the back.

Repeat this three more times (always increasing after the first 6 sts on the first needle and before the last 6 sts on the second needle). Cast off all the sts except the 6 at the back. With these K 14 rows. Cast off. Knit the other leg likewise.

For the arm cast on 15 sts in the colour of the jumper. K 24 rounds. Change to face colour and K 6 rounds. Break yarn and thread through the sts using a darning needle. Pull together tightly and sew in securely on the wrong side. Knit the other arm in the same way. For the hat cast on 40 sts. Purl one round. K 14 rounds. Dec. 1 st at the beginning and at the end of the next and every alternate round. When only 4 sts are left, break yarn and thread through the sts. Pull together tightly and sew in securely on the wrong side. If you wish, make a pom-pom (see p.138) and fix it at the end of the hat. Close off feet by sewing the heelpiece to the frontpiece.

Stuff the body, including the head, quite firmly. Draw the top of the head together by threading some wool through the edge.

Thread some wool through the neckline and draw together to shape the head.

Stuff the arms. Close the ends and sew them onto the body. Pull some wool around the wrists and draw together to make the hands. Put the hat on the head and sew it on with small stitches. Using the same technique for making the hair as described for finger puppets (p.97) make some hair around the edge of the hat. Embroider a face if wished (see under Dolls).

102
Bird table

It is important for children to finish a project once started and not to end up with many half made things. This bird table can be made in a short time and it is exciting for the child to watch the birds feeding from it.
If there is only a little time, some thin rope can be bought and used instead of making one's own cords with string.
(If plywood is used, make sure it is external ply.) Our six year old son enjoyed drilling the holes with a big hand-drill best!

Instructions:

Sand the piece of wood until it is nice and smooth. Depending on the shape of the wood, drill three or four holes about 2cm (¾") from the edges.

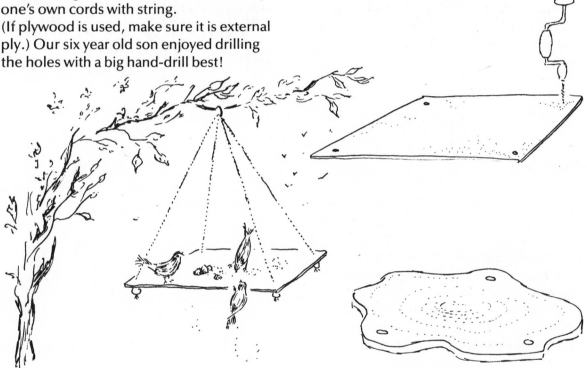

You will need:

One piece of wood, about 30cm (12") square or a slice of tree trunk of similar size
A ball of string for cords (or 2.8m (9ft) thick rope)
Drill and 12mm(½") drill bit

With the string make three or four lengths (about 70cm (27½") long each) of cord (see p.16). Thread each cord through one of the holes. Make a knot underneath the board at the end of each cord to stop the cords slipping out. Gather the cords together at the top and make a knot.
Hang your bird table outside the window.

103
The camp

The camp has been for years one of the most favourite toys for imaginative play in our households. It provides the walls for the children's playhouse. Planks, veils, sheets or tablecloths can all be used to make the roof of this easy-to-construct secret corner. Last, but not least, although it is fairly large when in use, it folds up and hardly takes up any storage space.

You will need:

Ten pieces of wood, each 70 x 3 x 2cm (27 x 1⅛ x ¾") for the uprights
Ten pieces of wood each 50 x 3 x 2cm (20 x 1⅛ x ¾") for the horizontals
Saw, chisel and hammer

Twenty screws
Woodglue
Sandpaper
String
Five pieces of material each 85 x 50cm (33½ x 20"), preferably in golden yellows and reds

Instructions:

Cut the wood as indicated.

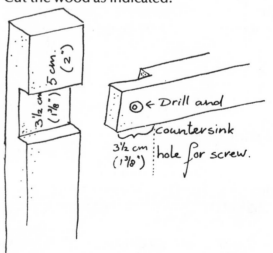

5 cm (2")
3½ cm (1⅜")

⊙ ← Drill and countersink hole for screw.
3½ cm (1⅜")

Sand down the edges until smooth. Assemble each frame 'dry'. If everything fits together tightly, number each joint and pull apart again. Keep the wood for each frame separate.

Now make the cloth covering.
Neaten the sides. Fold under approx 11½ cm (4½") at the top and bottom and make seams wide enough for the horizontal slats to slide through. Slide the slats through the seams and assemble each frame with its own cloth panel and see if the material fits tightly on the frame. If it is too slack, take up the material in a ruffle at the top.

After testing each frame and its cloth panel, pull apart the joints, leaving the cloth on the cross bars. Now glue and screw each joint. Finally assemble the frames by tying them together as shown.

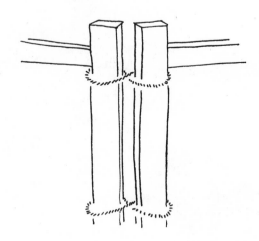

104
Coconut cradle and birdfeeder

A coconut can be transformed into a rocking cradle for all those tiny dolls that get lost so easily in a child's bed. An older child could knit a tiny blanket and make some bedding for the cradle from scraps of material fitted with a bit of cotton wool or fleece. Alternatively, if we turn the coconut the other way round we just need to drill a hole in one end and it will be ready to hang outside the window as a birdfeeder. Not only can you make lovely gifts, but you will also be able to enjoy eating the contents of the coconut.

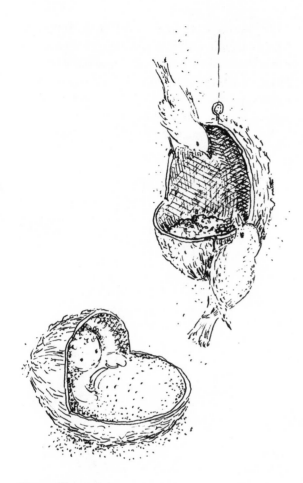

Then stand the coconut on end and saw down to meet the first cut.

Take out the edible bit of the coconut and the rocking cradle is ready.
For the birdfeeder, drill a small hole at the top and thread some string through for hanging it up.

105
Potato print

To get a pleasing overall design you only need a very simple printing shape. The grouping of the prints on the paper is important. Bear in mind what you are using the print for: perhaps a card to send to a friend, a bookcover or a border for a doll's house? You can make your own wrapping paper by printing onto lining paper.

You will need:

One coconut
A hacksaw for cutting it

Instructions:

Drain the liquid out of the coconut by piercing two of the dark depressions at one end. To stop the coconut from rolling about while cutting it, place it on the frog of a brick (the hollow side).
With a hacksaw carefully cut halfway through the waist of the coconut as shown.

You will need:

A medium size potato
A small knife
A bit of watercolour paint squeezed and
flattened out onto a plate
Cartridge (drawing) paper
Piece of scrap paper

Instructions:

Cut the potato in half.
Design the print : the simpler the better.

Cut the background away from the design to
a depth of about ½cm (¼").

Press the printing surface onto the paint and
try out the print on a small piece of scrap
paper. Adjust paint or shape if necessary.
Now the real work starts. Print the shape on
the cartridge paper as evenly as possible in a
neat pattern bearing in mind what you want
the print for. Some examples:

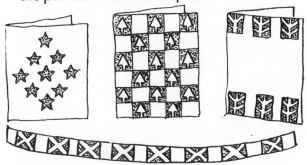

106
Coathanger cover

This is a good and simple way of using up
your wool leftovers and at the same time
making a nice present for someone!

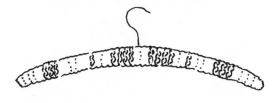

You will need:

20gr (¾oz) double knitting wool
One pair 3¾mm (4 US) knitting needles
One wooden coathanger (see illustration)

Instructions:

Cast on 14 sts and knit as many rows as you
need to cover the coathanger, in garter
stitch (about 42cm (16½") long).
Cast off.
Sew in any loose ends.
Find the centre of the knitted piece and slide
it over the metal hook of the coathanger.
Sew together the edges of the cover all
around the coathanger.

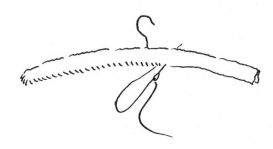

107
Needle case

This is an ideal project for a child who has just learned to knit. This knitting can be done in various colours, is very simple and will not go on and on! It makes a nice present for anyone who uses needles and pins.

Attach a short cord (see p.16) to the middle of each side of the knitted piece so that the case can be tied and closed. You may now fill the 'book pages' with pins and sewing needles.

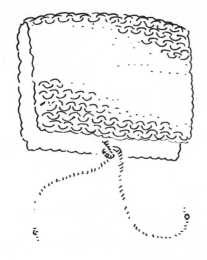

You will need:

Scraps of double knitting wool
One pair of 3¾mm (4 US) knitting needles
Two pieces of felt about 12 x 8cm (4¾ x 3")
each. (The colours of the felt should match
the colours of the wool)

Instructions

Cast on 20 stitches and knit 60 rows in garter stitch. Cast off. Sew in threads. Lay the two pieces of felt on top of the knitted piece and sew down the middle, using a running stitch.

108
Card stand

Sometimes one receives a very beautiful card: for instance a good reproduction. To do it justice and display it nicely, and not just prop it up against another object, you can use this card stand.
The very young woodworkers can make this as a first project. They can do it so easily that we found the whole family was provided for very quickly!

You will need:

A small off-cut 15 x 2 x 2cm (6 x 1 x 1") of softwood
A saw
A plane or rasp
Sandpaper, medium and fine
Linseed oil and a rag for putting it on

Instructions:

Cut the wood the right size. With the plane or rasp, take away the rough edges. This can be done very simply by just rounding the two top edges off, or in a slightly more difficult way, by making sloping surfaces.

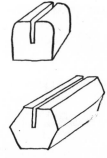

Make a cut as shown. This might need extra supervision. This cut takes the card. Sand down again any sharp splinters.
Lastly, oil the piece sparingly several times, to bring out the grain.

109
Woven pencil case

A woven pencil case can be a lovely present for Mum or Dad, or a good friend. It is simple to make and very rewarding.

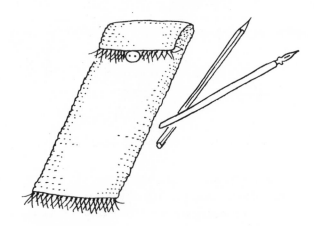

You will need:

Firm card 25 x 10cm (10 x 4")
Sharp scissors or a craft knife
Small balls (left-overs) of wool in matching colours
A small leftover of thin wool
Extra strong wool, like rug-making wool for the warp
Large embroidery needle

Instructions:

Cut teeth out of the card on both narrow sides, as shown.

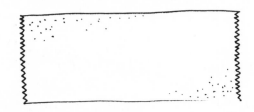

Put the warp on, as shown, covering front and back.

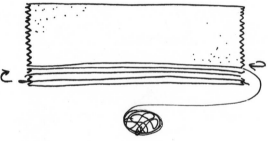

Continue weaving until you have approx. 17cm (7") of weaving. Then stop weaving on the front and only weave further on the back. Do this for another 3cm (1¼"). This is the flap. Cut the warp furthest away from the weaving.

Now the weaving can begin.

Start the weaving with a few rows of thin wool to prevent the end from fraying. Start 3cm (1¼") away from the end.

Weave, and this is the unusual element, on the front as well as the back. Your first row is on the front, then turn over the card and continue to weave on the back. Turn it back again for the second row on the front etc. This way you make a tube. Push the weaving firmly together, so that it makes a firm piece of cloth.

Knot the warp as shown.

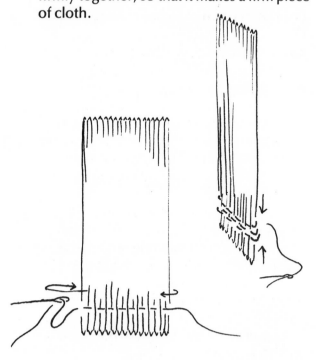

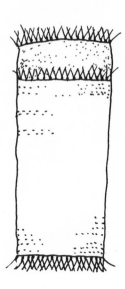

You can sew the warp back in if you like, or you can leave it. Fold the flap over and make a loop.

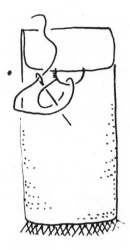

To finish off you sew a button onto the case to hold the loop.

110
Jacob's ladder

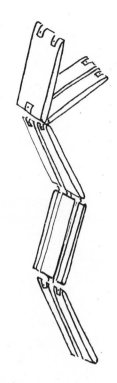

This is a very old and ingenious toy. When the top is turned, the block falls and appears to pass rapidly down first one side and then on the other, until it reaches the bottom. But the eye is easily deceived. Although it is simply made, it needs some figuring out to start with.

You will need:

Seven or more (twelve is a good number) wooden blocks 10 x 6½ x 1cm (4 x 2½ x ⅜")
Rasp and/or sandpaper
Tape 13mm (¼") wide
Scissors
Glue
Tacks & hammer
Watercolour & brush

Instructions:

Round off the edges of the blocks and smooth them down with sandpaper.
Cut the tape into strips long enough to cover one length, the back of one block and part of the front – see picture. There are three tapes to each block. Glue and nail tape (a) to the centre of the upper end of block A. Bring it over and down to the centre of block B and fix.
Tapes (b) and (b) are now fastened to the opposite end of A, about ½cm (¼") away from the end on either side. Bring these around the opposite end of B, as shown. The centre tape (c) is fastened to B and then brought down underneath to the centre of the opposite end of (c). The tapes must be arranged like this throughout the whole set of blocks.

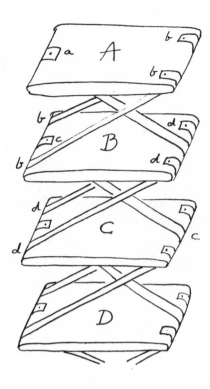

When finished, hold the blocks as seen in Diagram 1. The top block A must be turned so as to bring the second block to the same level. The top of this block then falls and it appears to pass quickly down, first on one side and then on the other until it reaches the bottom. But what really happens is that the second block becomes reversed and falls back again in its former position. This makes it come level with the third block, which at once falls over on the fourth and so on to the end of the ladder.

To heighten the effect, the blocks should be coloured. Use complementary colours for the opposite sides.

111
Small presents

Buy some seeds or collect your own in the Autumn. Wrap a few in tissue paper. Staple them onto a written description of what to do with them. Let the result be a surprise.

Our four year old received a marvellous birthday present from his girlfriend. It was a large opened up pinecone which had a Smarty on every scale. What a pretty, delicious thing!

112
Valentine hearts

Using soft reds and blues for the felt, this is a very attractive mobile for St Valentine's Day.

You will need:

61cm (2ft) of dowelling, or some small thin branches
Red and blue cotton
Two squares of red felt 23 x 23cm (9 x 9")
Two squares of pale blue felt 23 x 23cm (9 x 9")
Glue

Now glue the four pairs of red hearts and three pairs of blue hearts together.

Sew a 10cm (4") length of cotton to each heart. Taking a piece of 7½cm (3") dowelling, tie one red heart and one blue heart to each end. Repeat with the other 7½cm (3") piece. Take the 15cm (6") length of dowelling, and tie on two red hearts and one blue one in the middle. Now attach a 10cm (4") length of cotton to each end of the 30cm (11¾") length of dowelling. Tie them to the middle of each 7½cm (3") length. Take a 61cm (2ft) piece of cotton and tie it first to the middle of the 30cm (11¾") length of dowelling and then to the middle of the 15cm (6") length of dowelling.

Now your mobile is ready to hang up.

Instructions:

Cut the dowelling into one 30cm (11¾") length, two 7½cm (3½") lengths and one 15cm (6") length.

Cut out eight 5cm (2") high hearts from the red felt, and six from the blue felt.

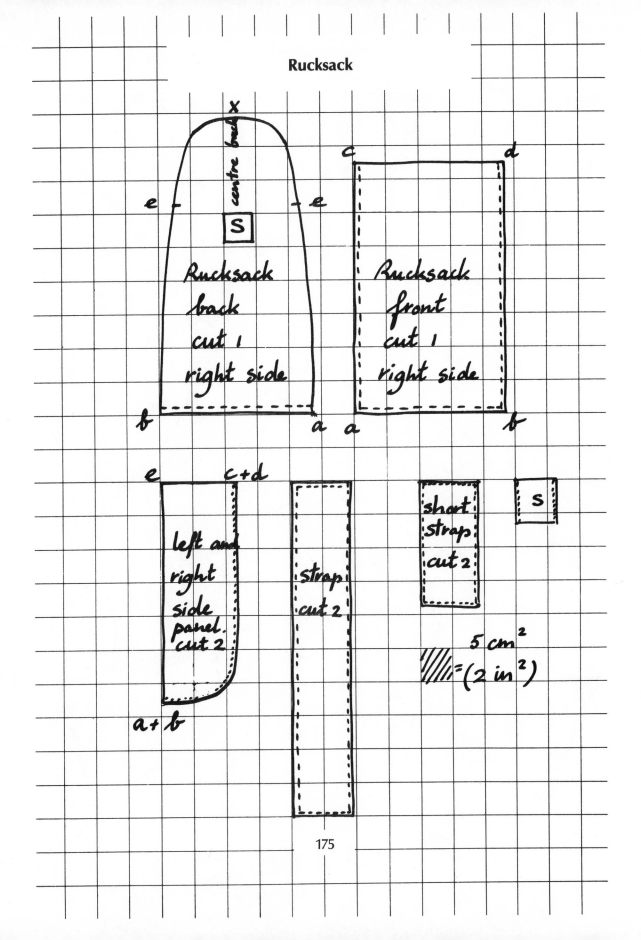

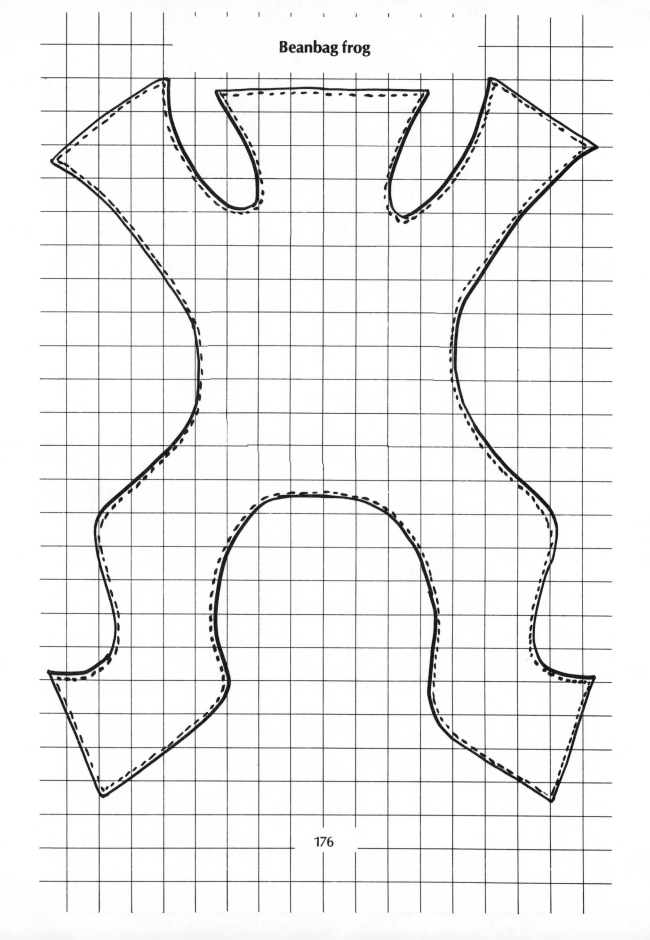

Baby's jumpsuit

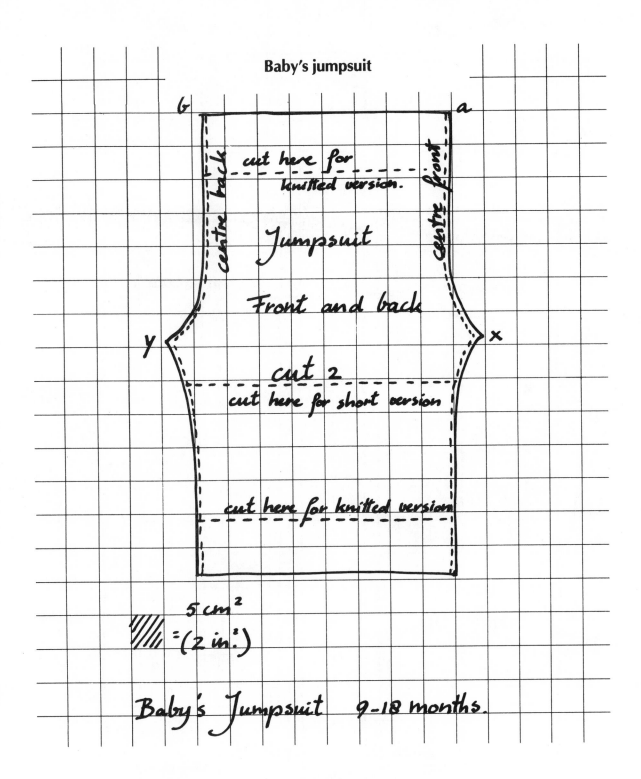

centre back

cut here for
knitted version.

Jumpsuit

Front and back

centre front

cut 2

cut here for short version

cut here for knitted version

5 cm²
= (2 in.)

Baby's Jumpsuit   9-18 months.

177

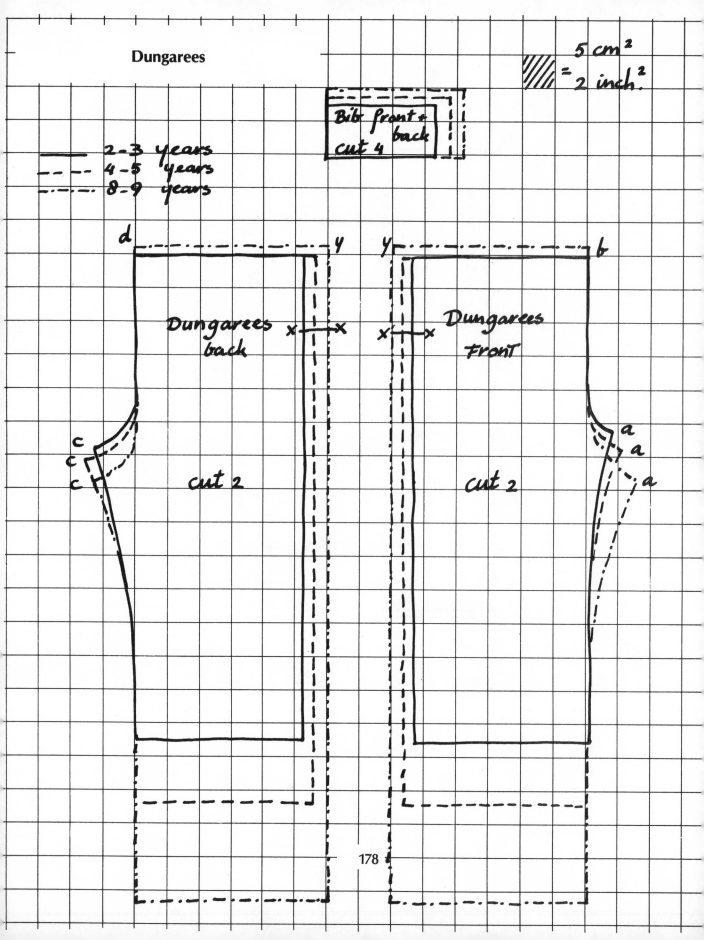

Dungarees

5 cm² = 2 inch²

——————— 2-3 years
— — — — 4-5 years
—·—·—·— 8-9 years

Bib front + back
cut 4

Dungarees back

Dungarees Front

cut 2

cut 2

d

y   y

b

x — x   x — x

c
c
c

a
a

a

Baby's sunbonnet

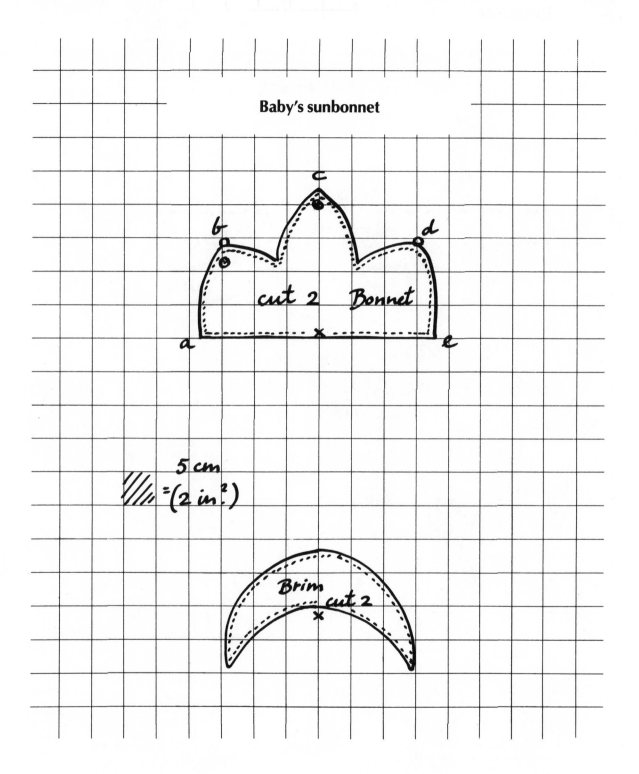

cut 2   Bonnet

5 cm = (2 in.²)

Brim cut 2

Toddler's sunhat

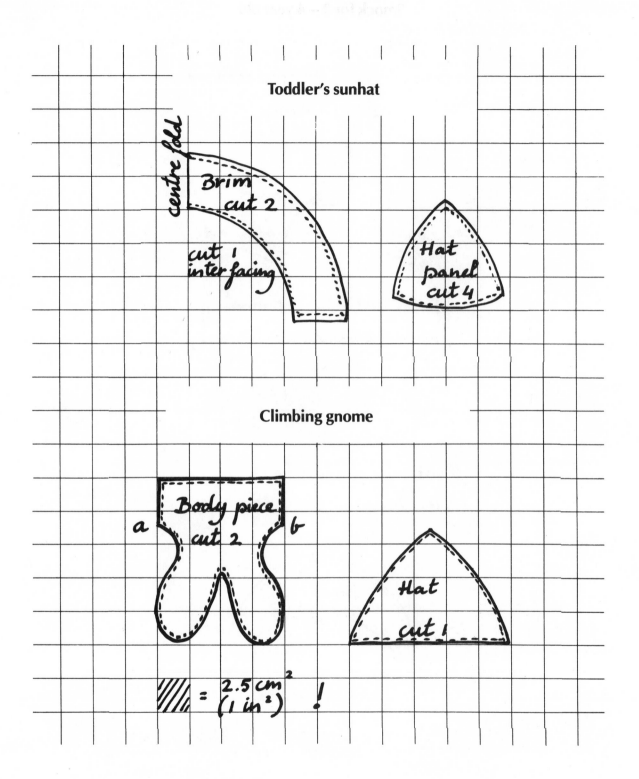

centre fold

Brim
cut 2

cut 1
inter facing

Hat
panel
cut 4

Climbing gnome

a   Body piece
cut 2   b

Hat
cut 1

▨ = 2.5 cm²
(1 in²) !

Smock for 3 – 4 year old

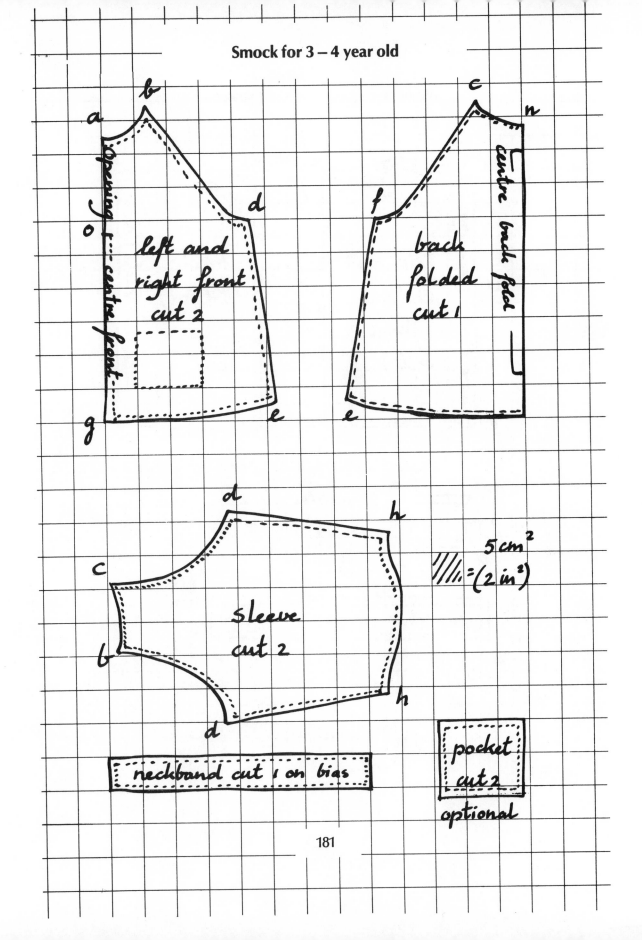

left and right front
cut 2

Opening – centre front

back folded
cut 1

centre back fold

sleeve
cut 2

$5\,cm^2$
$=(2\,in^2)$

neckband cut 1 on bias

pocket
cut 2
optional

181

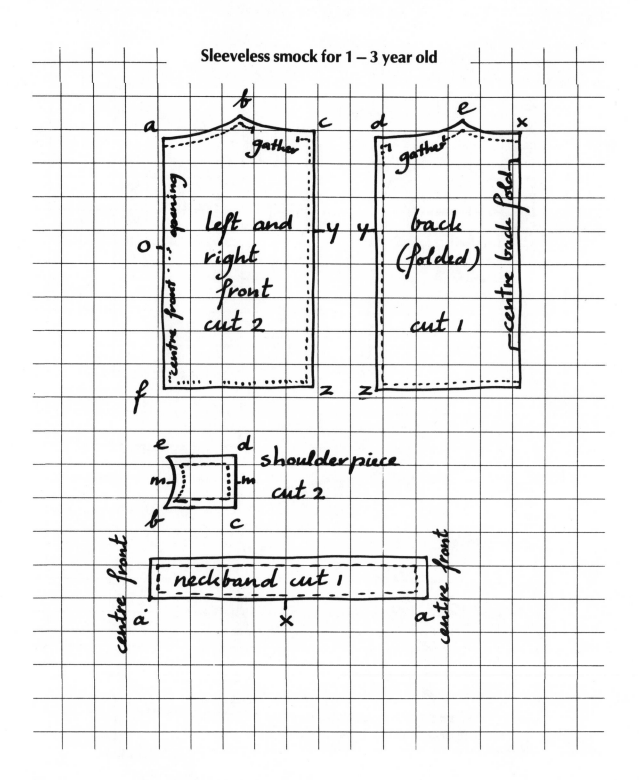

Jacket for 2 – 3 year old

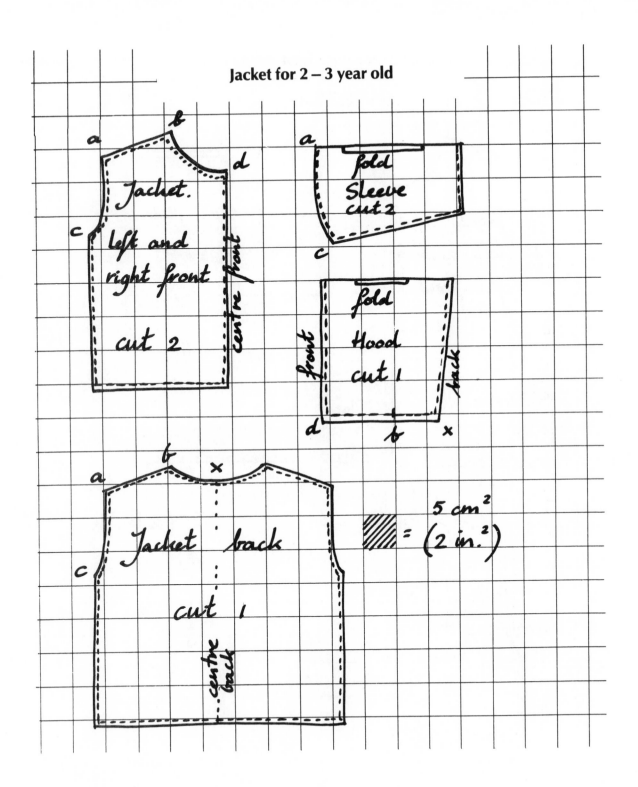

Jacket.
left and right front
cut 2

centre front

a   b   d

c

Sleeve cut 2
fold

a

c

Hood cut 1
fold

front

back

d   b   x

Jacket back
cut 1

b   x

a

c

cut 1

centre back

5 cm² = (2 in.²)

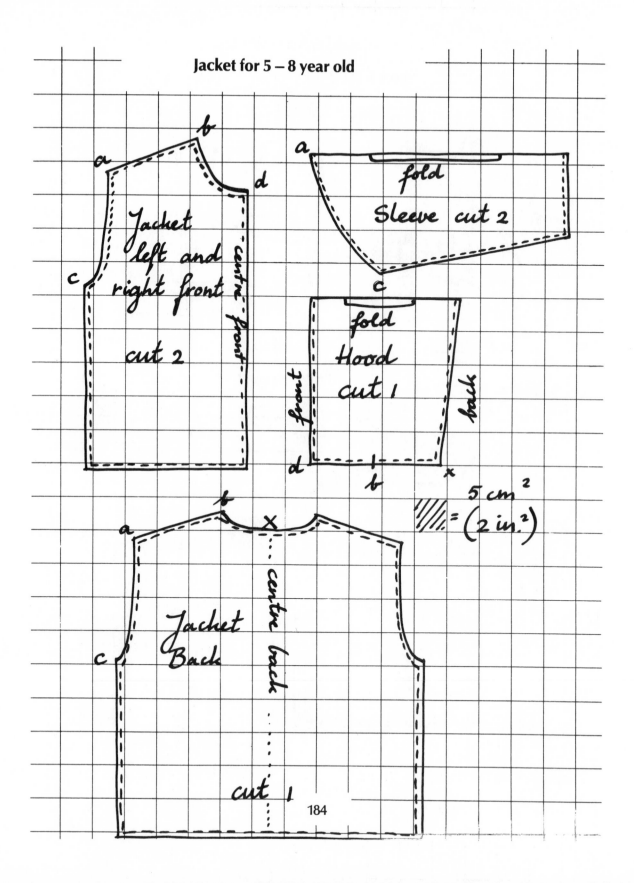

Jacket for 5 – 8 year old

a b

Jacket
left and
right front

cut 2

centre front

c

d

a fold
Sleeve cut 2

c

fold
Hood
cut 1

front

back

d

b x

5 cm²
= (2 in.²)

b X

a

Jacket
Back

centre back

c

cut 1

184

Baby's and toddler's sleeping bag

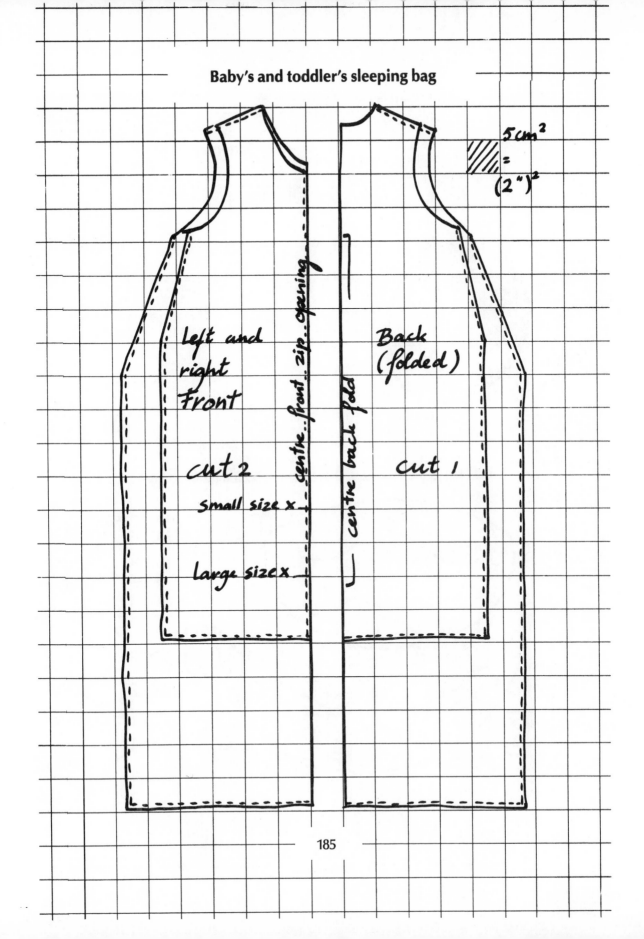

5 cm² = (2")²

Left and right Front

cut 2

Small size x

Large size x

centre front zip opening

centre back fold

Back (folded)

cut 1

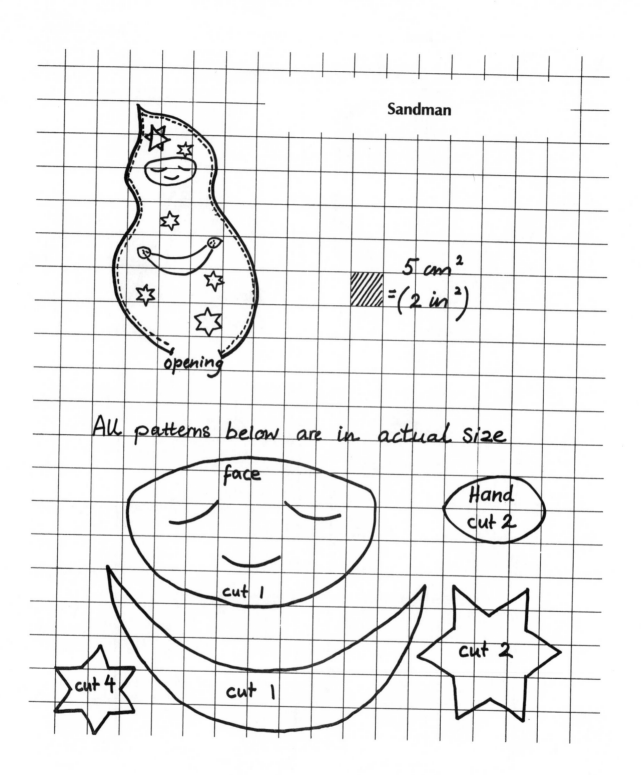

5 cm^2
$= (2 \text{ in}^2)$

All patterns below are in actual size

face

cut 1

Hand
cut 2

cut 2

cut 4

cut 1

opening

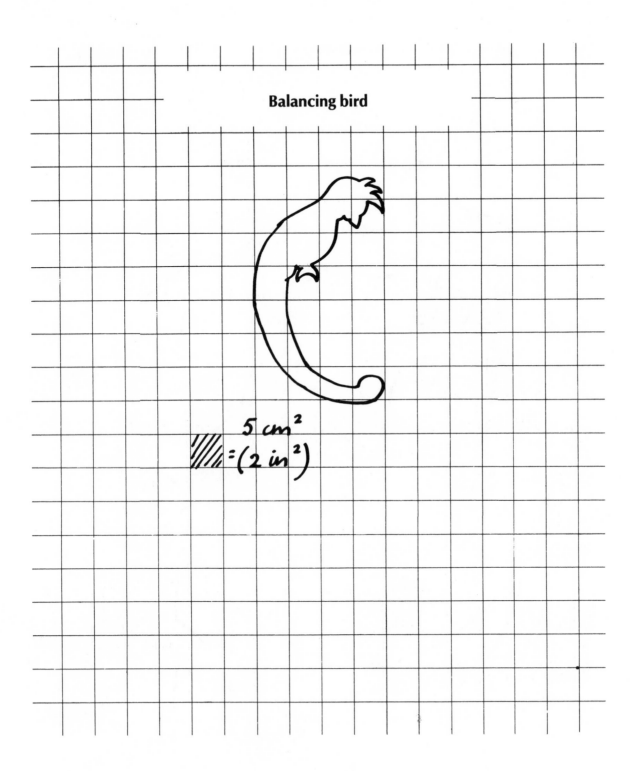

Balancing bird

5 cm²
= (2 in²)

Toddler's apron

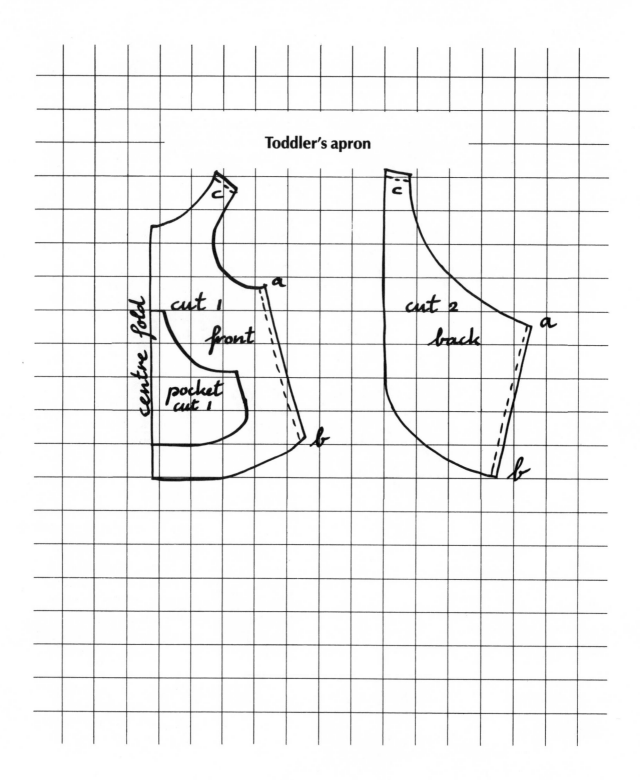

Acknowledgements

We particularly wish to thank Gerda Hillman, who put us on the right track, Pat Jones who gave us helpful advice, our children who created the need for us to be inventive, Veronica Loynes for her prompt typing, and Margaret Shillan for her visual advice.

The instructions and illustrations of Section 94 are reproduced with permission of Floris Books from Freya Jaffke, **Toymaking with Children** (formerly **Making Soft Toys**) and from Karin Neuschütz, **The Doll Book.**

The authors

Christine Fynes-Clinton was born in Switzerland and educated at the Zürich Steiner School. She is a music teacher and mother of four children. She has worked in occupational therapy and enjoyed craft-work since she was a child.

Marye Rowling was an art teacher in Holland before she came to study in England. Here she turned mother and housewife as well. Now she is trying to weave all these diverse threads into one tapestry.

Stephanie Cooper is a mother of five children. She ran a playgroup in Central London for some years, and since then has been interested and involved in setting up housing communities. In such a community she met Christine and Marye.

Bringing up young children in this situation gave many exciting possibilities for enriching both their families' and their personal lives. What can sometimes be a lonely and difficult time for parents, became for them a time of rich experience, celebrating festivals and making and doing things together. A mixture of nationalities living together enabled ideas, customs, songs, stories and recipes to be pooled and shared.

The ideas for this book have been gathered from many sources, but while compiling them the authors have often felt the urge to say "Do you remember when?".

FESTIVALS, FAMILY AND FOOD
Diana Carey and Judy Large.

"Packed full of ideas on things to do, food to make, songs to sing and games to play, it's an invaluable resources book designed to help you and your family celebrate the various festival days scattered round the year."

The Observer

Paperback; full colour cover;
10" × 8" (250 × 200mm);
216pp; over 200 illustrations.
ISBN 0 950 706 23 X
Fourth impression.

THE INCARNATING CHILD
Joan Salter.

Even in today's modern technological world, the mystery and miracle of conception, pregnancy and birth stir within many people a sense of wonder. **The Incarnating Child** picks up Wordsworth's theme "our Birth is but a sleep and a forgetting . . ." and follows the Soul life of tiny babies well into childhood. It is full of practical advice for mothers, fathers, relations or anyone concerned with childcare. Joan Salter examines pregnancy, birth, early infancy, babyhood, childhood, on up to adolescence. She addresses physical and spiritual development, the formation of healthy personalities, nutrition, clothing, environment, toys and learning, immunization and health, and the acquisition of skills and thinking ability. She writes with an astounding attention to detail, and the voice of years of experience in her field.

Joan Salter is a specialist in maternal and childcare, and has a nursing background which included work with migrants from many countries. She is the founder and director of the Gabriel Baby Centre, since 1976 a centre for maternal and child welfare in Melbourne, and is essentially concerned with the upbringing of the child in the home.

Full colour cover; 8¼" × 5¼" (210 × 135mm);
220pp approx.; illustrations and photos.
ISBN 1 869 890 04 3

ARIADNE'S AWAKENING
Taking up the threads of consciousness.
Margli Matthews,
Signe Schaefer
and Betty Staley.

Much has been written about women and men in terms of rôles, gender and social forms through the ages. The past two decades have witnessed widespread change in 'rights' and 'equality' on external levels, but this has not always made for more human fulfillment. The authors acknowledge the context of feminism, but broaden its picture enormously. They view 'masculine' and 'feminine' not just as bodily forms, but as principles of meaning: principles at work within each of us, in society and indeed in the entire span of Earth evolution.

Ariadne's Awakening traces through myth and history the journey humankind has made up to the present; it considers phases of life, relationships for men and women, and confronts such issues as the scientific management of conception and death, the rape of Earth's natural resources and the need for a New Feminine to influence values and decisions for the future.

Ariadne's Awakening is a book about understanding ourselves, and a search for a creative balance.

Signe Schaefer teaches at the Waldorf Institute, Spring Valley, New York. Margli Matthews teaches at Emerson College, Sussex and Betty Staley teaches in California. Signe and Margli were founder menbers of the Ariadne Women's Group, and wrote articles for **Lifeways**.

Sewn limp bound; 8¼" × 5¼" (210 × 135mm);
220pp approx.
ISBN 1 869 890 01 9

WHO'S BRINGING THEM UP?
Television and child development.
Martin Large.

Second edition.
To be published in German.

BETWEEN FORM AND FREEDOM
A practical guide to the teenage years
Betty Staley

Between Form and Freedom offers a wealth of insights about teenagers. There are sections on the nature of adolescence – the search for the self, the birth of intellect, the release of feeling, male-female differences and character. Teenager's needs are explored in relation to family, friends, schools, the arts and love. Issues such as stress, depression, drugs, alcohol and eating disorders are included.

Betty Staley has taught literature with teenagers for many years. She teaches at the Sacramento Waldorf School, runs workshops, serves on the Rudolf Steiner College faculty and wrote for **Ariadne's Awakening**. Her children are now grown up.

"In this excellent book, Betty Staley has given us a compassionate, intelligent and intuitive look into the minds of children and adolescents. Even the most casual reader of this book will never again respond to children and adolescents in the old mechanical ways... Naively, one could only wish this work were a best seller. Practically, I can only hope it will be read by a significant number of significant people – namely, parents, teachers, and, indeed, adolescents themselves."

Joseph Chilton Pearce
author of **The Magical Child**

Full colour cover; 215 x 138mm;
224pp; 5 black and white drawings;
ISBN 1 869 890 08 6
To be published 1st September 1988

LIFEWAYS
Working with family questions.
Gudrun Davy and Bons Voors.

Lifeways is about children, about family life, about being a parent. But most of all it is about freedom, and how the tension between family life and personal fulfillment can be resolved.

"These essays affirm that creating a family, even if you are a father on your own, or a working mother, can be a joyful, positive and spiritual work. The first essay is one of the wisest and balanced discussions of women's rôles I have read."

Fiona Handley,
Church of England Newspaper.

Paperback; colour cover;
6" × 8¼" (150 × 210mm); 316pp.
ISBN 0 950 706 24 8
Third impression 1985.
Lifeways is published in German and Dutch.

ORDERS

If you have difficulties ordering from a bookshop you can order direct from Hawthorn Press, Bankfield House, 13 Wallbridge, Stroud, GL5 3JA, U.K. Telephone 045 36 - 77040

TO A DIFFERENT DRUMBEAT
A practical guide to parenting children with special needs
P. Clarke, H. Kofsky, J. Lauruol

"If a man does not keep pace with his companions, perhaps it is because he hears a different drummer. Let him step to the music he hears, however measured or far away"

Henry David Thoreau

Most of us ask instinctively at the moment of giving birth – "Is she all right?" or "Is he all there?", wanting reassurance that the newborn is a "perfect" human being. The majority of parents receive positive answers. For those who do not, a life journey to uncharted places begins. There is uncertainty, bewilderment, or grief. There can also be a gradual discovering of new forms of Wholeness, and the unique personality and individuality each child brings – regardless of handicap.

This is a book on practical childcare, with a difference. It is written by parents, for parents, and offers suggestions (based on experience) in such areas as sleep, feeding, incontinence, play, behaviour, growth, siblings, clothing, travel and more. It addresses the emotional needs and development of child and adult. *To a Different Drumbeat* seeks to enhance the process of caring for children who have special needs.

In an age dominated by illusions of perfection, increasing reliance on amniocentisis, and genetic engineering, the message here is a bold one: "Look what we can do. See how life and society are richer through diversity, and how much we can learn from our children." It is a message about growing, about loving, and about help in a specific area of parenting.

"A 'Doctor Spock' for parents of children with special needs."

Publication: May 1989; Lifeways Series; 240 pages; sewn limp bound; colour cover; line drawings; 246 × 189 mm; ISBN 1 869 890 094 Available from Hawthorn Press

TOYMAKING WITH CHILDREN
Freya Jaffke

The toys surrounding a child during his or her first five years are of great importance. They awaken the imagination and stimulate creativity. Out of her long experience as a kindergarten teacher Freya Jaffke makes numerous suggestions for making toys from wooden boats, log trains, dolls furniture to rag dolls, puppets and soft animals.

Sewn softback; illustrated
6¾" x 8¼" (21 x 17cm); 96 pages
ISBN 0 86315 069 1
Floris Books

THE DOLL BOOK
Soft dolls and creative free play
Karin Neuschütz

This book's first half discusses how children play at different ages, how they are affected by their environment and the people around them, and how disarmingly simple it can be for adults to play and grow with the children who have come to them. Its second half gives detailed instructions on how to make a variety of simple soft cloth dolls that activate the impulse toward imaginative free play in both child and adult.

Hardback or paperback; illustrated
5½" x 8½" (22 x 14cm); 178 pages
ISBN 0 86315 028 4 (hb); 0 86315 022 5 (pb)
Floris Books

If you have difficulty ordering Floris books from a bookshop you can order direct, quoting Visa or Access (Mastercard) number, from W & R Chambers, 43 Annandale Street, Edinburgh. EH7 4AZ Telephone 031-557 4571